Endorsements

Faith doesn't deny a problem's existence. It just denies it a place of influence. Rick Curry successfully writes from this mindset, aware of the challenge of the day but completely unimpressed with the powers of darkness. We can and must learn from him. *The Sound of Awakening* was written out of an encounter with the Lord. And to be honest, it's my favorite kind of book, as it is filled with hope, wisdom, and divine strategy. Read with great anticipation; his hope and wisdom are contagious.

BILL JOHNSON
Bethel Church
Redding, California
Author of *The Way of Life* and
Born for Significance

Fifteen years ago, Rick Curry walked into our sanctuary at Community Chɪ　　　　　　　　　cky. I asked him if he would ɪ　　　　　　　　　　irty minutes later he had del　　　　　　　　　ɪessage to our congregation　　　　　　　　　gate our journey of community transformation. From that day forward, we have established a true friendship.

Rick Curry has been given to the Body of Christ "for such a time as this." The book you have in your hand will encourage you, guide you, and help you understand about the perilous times that lie ahead.

Rick asks two questions: Are we entering the days of God's end-time awakening and revival? Are you ready to take your place in the unfolding of awakening and revival?

May you be stirred to action as you read this timely book!

Doug Abner
Appalachian Dawn
City of Hope

THE
SOUND OF
AWAKENING

THE
SOUND OF
AWAKENING

A PROPHETIC CALL FOR
EVERYDAY PEOPLE TO ARISE
AND RELEASE REVIVAL

RICK CURRY

DESTINY IMAGE® PUBLISHERS, INC.

P.O. Box 310, Shippensburg, PA 17257-0310

"Promoting Inspired Lives."

This book and all other Destiny Image and Destiny Image Fiction books are available at Christian bookstores and distributors worldwide.

Cover design by Eileen Rockwell

Interior design by Terry Clifton

For more information on foreign distributors, call 717-532-3040.

Reach us on the Internet: www.destinyimage.com.

ISBN 13 TP: 978-0-7684-5898-5

ISBN 13 eBook: 978-0-7684-5899-2

ISBN 13 HC: 978-0-7684-5901-2

ISBN 13 LP: 978-0-7684-5900-5

For Worldwide Distribution, Printed in the U.S.A.

1 2 3 4 5 6 7 8 / 25 24 23 22 21

Contents

Foreword

by Dutch Sheets

Never have I been more certain that America's only hope for recovery from her loss of strength and purpose is a Third Great Awakening, and never have I been more certain that such an awakening is coming. This great revival, however, won't occur only in America; it will be worldwide. In fact, earth's greatest harvest has now begun. Heaven is determined, prepared, and confident.

The Church, Christ's Ekklesia, is being readied and positioned for this epoch-making era. God is raising up leaders like Rick Curry to assist in this process and to pioneer the first wave. Prophetic forerunners who have the ability, just as Elijah did, to hear awakening's rumbling sound when it cannot yet be heard by others are now preparing the way. They do so with messages, of course, and also with books such as this. As spiritual tuning forks, their words tune us to the frequency of heaven, enabling our hearts to hear what they're hearing.

Not only do I love the title of this book, but I'm also thrilled with its subtitle: *A Prophetic Call for Everyday People to Arise and Release Revival*. In Acts, the early Church immediately began experiencing supernatural growth. Holy Spirit "added" to their number daily.

Frankly, the incredible growth was a bit overwhelming for this multiplying, unorganized body of believers. What a wonderful problem!

Then, in His infinite wisdom, Holy Spirit allowed the apostles' frustration to reach a point which motivated them to seek a new pattern. "Let's spread the responsibility somewhat," they said among themselves. "We'll appoint deacons to oversee the practical, hands-on responsibilities of pastoral care." They chose seven good men, full of faith and the Holy Spirit, laid hands on them, and commissioned them for the task (see Acts 6:1-6).

Holy Spirit had more in mind than the food program, however, as important as that was. When the apostles laid hands on the deacons, an impartation of power, anointing, and the gifts of Holy Spirit occurred. The same anointing carried by the apostles to preach the gospel and heal the sick was transferred to the deacons! As they distributed food and clothing, they also distributed the power of God. Incredible signs and wonders began occurring through them as well as the apostles, and a new era in church history was born. This new body of Christ realized that the ministry of preaching the gospel with signs following wasn't just for a select group of leaders; it was for all believers, just as Jesus had said in Mark 16:15-19.

Game changer!

A little-known fact regarding this change occurred in Acts 6 after the deacons were anointed. From this point on, the growth of the Church was no longer described as Holy Spirit *adding* to their numbers. Throughout the remainder of the book of Acts the descriptive term changed to *multiplied!* When those empowered to preach and pray multiplied from leaders alone to the body as well, the harvest did also.

Get ready for déjà vu!

This coming great awakening will not be released by leaders only but by all willing believers. It was never Christ's intent to only work through leaders. Certainly, leaders are needed to equip, coordinate, and govern; but the work of the ministry is intended for all believers. You, faithful brothers and sisters, are about to be promoted!

This powerful book by my friend, Rick Curry, will awaken faith in you for this next great awakening. But just as importantly, it will awaken *you*. In this next, greatest of all revivals, you're not called to warm the bench. God is calling your number, putting you in the game. There will be only one Superstar—Christ Himself. The rest of us will all be equal players, deflecting all glory to Him.

Get ready!

Introduction

An audible sound filled the two-hundred-year-old church. I immediately glanced to check the specific location of my wife as I was deeply concerned the old floor joists supporting the sanctuary floor were giving way under the capacity crowd that had gathered to contend for awakening in Kentucky and the nation. Some thought the sound was a sudden storm blowing through the region, but my attention first went toward the structure of the old building. Was this another sign in the unfolding storyline of God intervening once again in history and bringing us closer to a major national and global awakening?

Let me back up. The pastor of Mt. Carmel Christian Church in Bourbon County, Kentucky, had invited me to speak on the church's 200th anniversary. Mt. Carmel was started during the days of the great revival at the Cane Ridge Meetinghouse just a few miles away. Cane Ridge is the most celebrated site of the beginning of the Second Great Awakening in the nation even though there had been powerful outpourings of the Holy Spirit before the meeting at Cane Ridge in August 1801. I had been asked by the pastor to share on Sunday morning about the history of revival in Kentucky and Cane

Ridge as well as the history of Mt. Carmel Church. I was delighted to do so and approached the weekend with great excitement. I had arranged with the pastor to host a regional gathering of pastors and leaders that evening. The morning service was delightful and powerful. The evening gathering was an explosive move of God that birthed a revival in the community of Paris, Kentucky, that would last for a year.

Mt. Carmel Church sits stoically on the side of the road amid the beautiful rolling hills of Bourbon County. When we entered on that Sunday evening, the old church was packed to capacity and seemed to welcome her guests with great enthusiasm. Worship was remarkable, and the people were energized with expectancy. The atmosphere felt electric! While standing on the platform I began to hear a deep rumble sound that reverberated around the room. I knew the basement beneath the sanctuary was not a part of the original design of the church, and the men of the church had dug the basement out by hand. I immediately became alarmed that the sound could be the beams collapsing beneath the floor, but clearly it was not. The sound was as if God had thundered upon the land and had moved among us, opening once again the well of awakening in the region and the nation. What would become of this? What could this possibly mean? We knew we must continue in these meetings and allow the response of our lives be the appropriate response, but what was the appropriate response to this magnificent revelation?

We were already scheduled to speak at River of Life Ministries in Paris, Kentucky, a couple of days after these Sunday meetings. Pastors Keith and Krista Hampton had long labored in this region, contending for awakening in the land. We went for two scheduled services and the revival continued for the entire year following. It was a miraculous outpouring wherein we witnessed many lives saved, baptized, healed, and delivered. The fruit of that revival continues to be stewarded by pastors and leaders in innovative ways.

Was this sound of awakening a sign of greater things to come?

I want to invite you to take a journey into the unfolding story of awakening and transforming revival in the nations of the earth. These are remarkable days, and God is moving mightily in the hearts and lives of ordinary men and women to fulfill His covenant promise in the nations. Watch for everyday men and women who begin to arise and release revival. God has always chosen to use the ordinary ones, and I propose He is doing it again.

Could it be that we are living in the days of mighty visitation that generations before us dreamed were coming? In *The Sound of Awakening*, I take you on a journey and tell you stories of dramatic encounters and outpourings of the Holy Spirit as we mark the trail to America's next great awakening.

Watch for mighty outpourings through the lives of people you have never heard of before. Watch for unexpected men and women to awaken and arise into places of ministry that a few years ago they would never have imagined. Watch for gatherings in the most unlikely places and open fields becoming packed to capacity with a generation desperate for an encounter with God. Watch for incredible dreams and visions to come forth, and, more importantly, be stewarded into a place of bold expression and powerful breakthrough. Watch for the worship of the victorious to become louder than the violence of the wounded. The Lord is pouring out His Holy Spirit in a mighty end-time move of God producing awakening and transforming revival.

> *It will come about after this that I will pour out My Spirit on all mankind; and your sons and daughters will prophesy, your old men will dream dreams, your young men will see visions. Even on the male and female servants I will pour out My Spirit in those days* (Joel 2:28-29).

Watch for the spirit of prayer to rest upon the lives of the ordinary ones. There is an emerging generation of those who are choosing the Presence of God in a closet over the applause of people on a stage. You will hear of some of those here in *The Sound of Awakening*. History has been marked by the ordinary ones who surrender to the "Spirit of grace and supplication" as in Zechariah 12:10.

Watch for the spirit of faith to manifest in the lives of the ordinary ones. I remember hearing an international evangelist years ago saying, "The question is not whether America comes back to God, but the question is will America come back to God by revelation or by desperation?" Let us be reminded that millions of people have lived in desperation throughout history, but *hope* is born amid an authentic revival wherein the masses turn back to God in faith.

Watch for the spirit of surrender to transform the lives and futures of multitudes. The early Church was surrendered to God, and His purposes were being boldly accomplished. In Acts 3:12 Peter reassured the onlookers, "Why look so earnestly on us, as though by our own power or holiness we had made this man walk?" The foundational pillars of humility, honor, and holiness will once again become the benchmarks for Christian ministry and service in this move of God.

Watch for the spirit of a quickening word to bring clear revelation that unlocks ministries, communities, and families and restores the purpose of God in the lives of people. In *The Sound of Awakening* I offer you incredible accounts of God moving suddenly through a quickening word to bring about another piece of the puzzle to America's next great awakening.

Watch for the spirit of fullness to be poured out in another dynamic expression of the outpouring of the Holy Spirit as in the book of Acts and at integral times throughout history. The Lord is going to remarry the purity and power in this awakening.

Let's go!

No more delay!

It's time for America's next great awakening. The nations will run into the glory of God and discover there a mighty refuge of hope and holiness.

Chapter 1

An Emerging Generation

And suddenly there came a sound from heaven as of a rushing mighty wind, and it filled all the house where they were sitting (Acts 2:2 KJV).

What on earth is happening? We are living in amazing days, and the Lord is again releasing the sound of awakening through the hearts and lives of ordinary men and women. Are we on the brink of another powerful awakening that will witness millions of men and women being born into the Kingdom of God?

Where would we begin to hear such hope? Hope is often hidden deeply within the harsh restraints and the bitter confines of unsuspecting people in the most unlikely places. We often refer to these, whom God chooses to use wildly, as the "ordinary ones." The description is simply to remind us of the amazing truth that God, the Holy Spirit, loves to use everyday folks— shepherds like David or Moses, tent-makers like Apostle Paul, fishermen like Peter, a cloth merchant like Lydia, an ordinary peasant girl named Mary, and a carpenter to save the world. Simple, ordinary people accomplish extraordinary exploits in the Kingdom of God.

Extraordinary Power

Consider that the Holy Spirit promised by the Father through Jesus is the Spirit of extraordinary power! "You will receive power when the Holy Spirit comes upon you" (Acts 1:8 NLT). The Greek word here for *power* is *dunamis,* from which we derive the word *dynamite!*

This world-changing hope was hidden in a boy who sang for his breakfast. Filled with utter despair, the young boy made his way through the wintry morning, offering to sing for a morsel of bread. He stood in front of the Cottas' home, but it appeared no one was stirring in the early hours of this bitterly cold morning. Suddenly, "Sing, boy! Sing! The ages are waiting for you. Sing! Sing! All the world will hear you. God knows what will come of it." So, the young lad raised his clear voice on this crisp morning and the lady of the house, Ursula Cotta, beckoned him to come inside for a warm breakfast. She had recognized him from the church choir and had noted his remarkable voice. She would care for him like a mother from that time forward.[1] None could have perceived at that time the hope that lay inside the young Martin Luther and the way God would use him to birth the mighty Protestant Reformation.

Awakening was afoot in Martin Luther. Cumbersome and corrupt religious structures and systems shook at the sound of Luther's voice and were radically transformed by his words of grace. Today, there is a hope that lies hidden in an emerging generation that waits in the shadows to be summoned by the Holy Spirit to take their place in the flow of salvation history. Their voices, quickened by the Holy Spirit, will be used mightily to awaken nations and impact future generations. Holy Spirit is summoning the hope within you and me now to reveal once again the heart of the Father to the lost.

Power for World Evangelism

The Holy Spirit, promised by the Father through Jesus, is the Spirit of power for world evangelism! "Ask of Me, and I will make the nations your inheritance and the ends of the earth your possession" (Ps. 2:8 CSB).

My wife and I stood recently in the United States Capitol in Washington, DC with some wonderfully courageous members of Congress who are believing the Lord for a mighty spiritual awakening. They spoke and prayed passionately; one even laid his head over the podium and with the sound of a groaning for God to come and heal our land.

Members of Congress came before us one by one and shared a common message of hope. Their message was that God was moving in the nation's capital, and several even expressed the expectation that revival may come to Congress itself. They spoke with courage and conviction, encouraging us to remain faithful and watch for big things to come. I left Washington, DC more inspired than ever before, and more humbled to pray for the political leaders in Washington. Incredible things are happening all over the country! Could it be that prophetic dreams are coming true and that the clarion call for apostolic reformers to arise because of awakening is coming to the land? Could it be we are on the brink of a mighty move of God and He is infusing hope for His awakening that will reap the greatest harvest the world has ever seen?

Hope is often hidden deeply within the harsh restraints of unsuspecting people in the most unlikely places. These are the unsuspecting ones emboldened by the scope of unimaginable dreams and compelled to bold acts of courage in the face of utter despair. History is shaped by prophetic dreamers, and dreams and visions must be stewarded by wise apostolic reformers. We all, I propose, have a significant role to play in the unfolding of America's destiny and her greatest spiritual awakening.

John Huss (1369–1415) is an amazing figure in history as an early reformer of the Church in Europe. He was a scholar with great skill for articulating the truth of Scripture. God used John Huss in astonishing ways, and his life is still very much worth remembering and celebrating. Huss was greatly inspired by John Wycliffe's writings and would go on to become the rector of Bethlehem Chapel in 1402. Huss was martyred for his faith and the bold witness of courage in his life was faithfully demonstrated. He was burned at the stake in 1415! As the fire was lit beneath him, he began to prophesy about the coming of a great reformer who would "soar like an eagle." Further, he said that no one would stop the reformer who would come along in the next 100 years. This was an amazing prophetic utterance of the Holy Spirit! Was Martin Luther the eagle seen in the prophecy by John Huss? We are living in the innocuous shadow of the great Reformation, but it could be that we are standing at the precipice of another earth-shaking move of God that began in the heart of a young boy who sang for his breakfast.

Power to Be Pursued

The Holy Spirit promised by the Father through Jesus is the Spirit of power to be pursued!

It is not easy to faithfully steward what the Holy Spirit has deeply ministered through dreams and visions. It is, however, easier when we can place ourselves visually within the perspective of history and steward our moment in time. Perhaps we are living in days seen by those who have gone before us?

Revival spread in the early 20th century from Azusa Street in Los Angeles to Chicago, Illinois. A mighty outpouring of the Spirit came to Stone Church when Maria Woodworth-Etter began a series of revival meetings on July 2, 1913. As Christians prayed around the altar one evening, Maria Woodworth-Etter and others gave the following powerful prophecy and divine promise, which would occur within 100 years of the 1913 Chicago Visitation. She prophesied of this coming end-time revival, "We are not yet up to the fullness of the Former Rain, and when the Latter Rain comes it will far exceed anything we have seen!"

Rev. William Seymour, the leader of the Azusa Street Awakening, also prophesied that in 100 years there would be an outpouring of God's Spirit and His Shekinah Glory would be greater and farther reaching than what was experienced at Azusa. The news of this revival in Chicago is not new and neither are the prophetic utterances, but there exists a strong sense of the Holy Spirit that those prophecies are coming to pass. There are people who have tried to faithfully steward those words by keeping them relevant and fresh in their hearts. The Lord is about to visit the nations of the earth with a mighty visitation that will witness the salvation of millions into the Kingdom of God.

There is an emerging generation waiting in the shadows to be summoned by the Holy Spirit to take their place in the flow of salvation history. He is summoning them now and they will carry the standard, exposing once again the heart of the Father for the lost and the power of the Holy Spirit to bring the harvest to the revelation of Jesus. Hope is hidden in the remnant of the aborted generation. The great hope of the Father is being manifested in the hidden streams and flowing tributaries of the testimonies of ordinary people who having been fiercely making an "appeal to heaven" for an awakening that will yield the fruit of a mighty harvest.

The prophetic utterance of John Huss was afoot in Martin Luther. Well-fortified religious structures and systems would not just be shaken by his voice but would indeed be radically transformed by his devotion.

Could God bring revival to the nation's capital? Will we soon witness a series of unexpected events that will shape the nation for her greatest awakening? I want to introduce to you a dream that I had. This dream has been shared all over the world.

Appeal to Heaven: The Dream

I was approaching a building that reminded me of a bygone era. It was built in a much simpler time, and its attraction was luring me to come inside. I knew I must enter the building.

The inside was draped in a heavy darkness, and yet I was compelled to explore. I felt encouraged to enter in and survey the way things once were and will be again.

Immediately I raked the wall searching for a switch to turn on some lights. I followed the lengthy path along the wall to its end where a warm and gentle-spirited man greeted me kindly.

I asked him if he knew where a light switch was, and he told me the buildings had no electricity. However, he said the walls were constructed with large wooden panels that could open allowing light and wind to blow into the room. Of course, I wanted to open them.

The first panel was much larger than I supposed. I pushed it slowly and then propped it open with the large board attached to it. I turned to look into the room and found it to be considerably deeper and wider than I had determined.

I opened the second and the third panels and placed them side by side along the wall. Upon opening the third window I was suddenly aware that light and a vigorous wind flooded the room. I could now see a massive platform at the opposite end of the room, and I determined the room appeared to seat thousands of people.

I continued along that wall until I reached a far back corner and noticed what appeared to be countless risers as if for a great group of observers or maybe a choir. It would be the latter. Finally, as I continued around the room and completed the task of opening the windows, I gaped at the size and the scope of this ancient place.

A rustic simplicity added to the building's beauty and reminded me of an old tabernacle used during great camp meetings or healing crusades. The wind rushed in, giving it breath and life.

The sound was deeply moving and my bones seemed to resonate with it. It was noise, but it was not. It was penetrating yet pleasant, remarkable but undefinable. Make no mistake, however, it was increasing with great intensity. It sounded as if the whole world were summoning the wind with a united moan.

Unsure of the source of the sound or the significance of the wind, I stood at the front of the massive hall. I saw now it would seat tens of thousands, maybe as high as 25,000 or even 30,000 people. I stood alone, but not for long. The elderly gentleman approached me again. I saw him more clearly now, and recognized his countenance to be as endearing as his voice and gestures of kindness.

He came nearer to me and asked if I would like to see what would happen next. I quickly affirmed that I could hardly wait. He gestured toward the platform and placed a single chair near the leading edge of the massive stage. We made our way to the front of the large room. I noticed the large, arching bridge extending from one side to the other at the back.

With a gesture, the elderly gentleman invited me to be seated in the chair. I sat all alone gazing upon the room as my eyes roamed across the stage and over to the open windows. The sound continued to get louder as if it were coming my way.

Pilgrims, Puritans, and Pietists

Suddenly, movement outside the window to my immediate right caught my attention. I leaned forward and saw ancient ships pulling into a beautiful harbor outside the building. The ships were now docked, and as the people began to disembark the sound became overwhelming. The people were dressed very conservatively in black. I asked the man, "Who are these people?" He replied, "These are the Pilgrims, the Puritans, and the Pietists."

I watched as they made their way to the old auditorium where I was seated alone. They filed in very neatly defined rows, never acknowledging my presence. They were singing! I could tell the sound of their song was flowing upon the wind! I was hearing it in that great volume of sound I had been hearing since the beginning. However, they were not singing in competition with the sound; instead, they were singing in harmony with it.

They filed into the room very methodically, filling every seat row by row beginning at the front of the auditorium. They were right in front of me. After filling the seats, a great number of them rose up, went to the rear of the auditorium, and began to sit in the choir risers. They sang ancient songs beautifully in a unique dialect and cadence. Afterward, they sat down as one.

The Pioneers

The sound increased and again my attention was drawn to the outside of the building. In the dream I could hear clopping of horses and wagon wheels clanging across the land. I saw many carriages, surreys, and covered coaches of all kinds pulling up to the grounds next to the building. Children were playing and families were coming arm in arm. The sound continued to increase, and I realized the children and families, too, were singing, but their song did not conflict in sound or scope with the song of the previous group. It was simply as if they were singing identically the same song in varying lyrical styles, but it was perfectly harmonious! I felt I was, for the first time, watching the gathering of generations.

I asked the gentleman, "Who are these people?" He replied, "These are the pioneers." When they entered the auditorium, the previous group stood and began to release a tremendous shout of welcome! They began to twirl and dance. The sound was exuberant and joyful. Upon entering the auditorium, they began to fill up row after row of seats. There were many of them! In a similar fashion after all were seated, some exited their places in order to join those on the massive choir risers at the rear of the auditorium.

The Planters

I could then hear another group approaching. They were driving very early automobiles of all sorts. I saw what looked like Model As and many other types. They were pulling onto the grounds next to the auditorium. I could distinctly hear the clattering of the early engines. Meanwhile, the sound in my dream still constantly increased.

I asked the gentleman beside me, "Who are these people?" He answered me and said, "These are the planters. They have labored to build cities and factories of all kinds. They have built communities, schools, churches, and many wonderful inventions have come from them."

The Synergy of the Ages

As this group began to make their way into the auditorium, the two previous groups stood as one people and began to clap and cheer, to dance and twirl around. They, too, came singing and their song, though unique from the two previous groups, seemed to flow seamlessly and harmoniously with the others. The sound continued to increase, and it was at this point I felt I was listening to the anthem of the ages. The song of the Spirit interpreted by the inspiring voices of each generation was being sung again in this magnificent old auditorium.

This group methodically took their seats, continuing to fill the auditorium full of both people and praise. I paused to look outside through the open windows, and I was inspired by the modes of transportation represented by the ancient ships in the harbor to the line of very first automobiles interspersed with wagons and surreys. I noted that the modes of transportation were a very key component of the dream.

The Prophets

Suddenly, I heard a distinct sound—a loud sound—of a new people arriving. Even though no specific dates were associated with any of the groups of people, I recognized many cars pulling up, like Packards, Pierce-Arrows, Oldsmobiles, and Thunderbirds from the early 20th century through the 1960s. This group stood out to me in the dream, because they seemed to be much more diverse and independent. I inquired of the gentleman, "Who are these people? They look and sound different from the others." He replied, "These are the prophets. The uniqueness of their times will cause them to begin to define the world for generations to come." I have come to believe, since the dream, that this truly was one of the most prophetic times in our history.

As they made their way into the auditorium, each of the previous groups stood to welcome them with song and dance. It was a beautiful and joyous celebration. As I sat on the platform observing, I was overwhelmed by the wonderful sights.

The prophets filed in and found their seats as methodically as the previous groups. They too had a large selection of people who went and joined the others in the large choir risers in the back. I recall in the dream I thought this might be the last group to appear as there seemed to be a distance in time between this group and the next. Then suddenly, they came!

The Pragmatists

I saw a commotion outside the auditorium and realized very modern and sophisticated modes of transportation began to flood onto the grounds. Modern cars were arriving, planes landing, helicopters making a sound as they battered the wind. At this point I was fully aware of the complete spectrum of modes of transportation, from ancient ships to the millions of dollars' worth of sophisticated planes, trains, and automobiles.

I inquired again of the gentleman, "Who are these people?" He replied, "These are the pragmatists." I have since had to search and determine an understanding of this by the Holy Spirit.

Upon entering the auditorium, all the previous groups shouted with a voice of triumph! It was a shout unlike any shout I had heard in the dream. After an extended time of celebration, they found their seats all over the auditorium. It was inspiring to watch pilgrims and pioneers dancing with each of the generations that came after them.

Are You Ready to Take Your Place?

The gentleman came to me once again while seated on the platform and instructed me to watch. He pointed toward the rear of the platform. The very large double doors opened on their own, and I could see ministers wearing the same attire as the first group and its era. The gentleman gestured to me and asked, "Are you ready to take your place?" The question pierced my spirit!

Suddenly, I saw my friend, Apostle Dutch Sheets, enter the room, and so I stepped into the line of some notable leaders. As we made our way center stage, Dutch took his position at the center of the bridge extending over the platform and began to wave a flag in a figure eight over the people. He released a powerful prophetic word over the gathering. I had never seen the flag before. It had a white background with an evergreen tree and writing on it.

The next morning as I sat alone in our home journaling about the dream, my wife, Jennifer, asked me if the flag was real. I assured her it was not, but she insisted we should research it. We discovered it was the historical "Washington's cruisers" flag, commonly referred today as the *Appeal to Heaven* flag. What could these things possibly mean? What was the Lord saying through this dream and the unfolding revelation and encounters we would experience in days to come?

This book is a small attempt at traversing the trail in search of the Lord's plan for awakening nations and reaping a mighty harvest of souls.

Note

1. Charles Carleton Coffin, *The Story of Liberty* (Harper & Brothers, 1878, 2018), 88-89.

Chapter 2

Voices upon the Wind

If my people who are called by my name humble themselves, and pray and seek my face and turn from their wicked ways, then I will hear from heaven and will forgive their sin and heal their land (2 Chronicles 7:14 ESV).

The short flight into Washington, DC was uneventful. We were on our descent, and I was pressed tightly against the window straining to get a glimpse of this exceptional city. The clouds began to morph into a shadowy gray color, and I was finally able to see the ground below. I peered past the streaks of rain streaming down the window. I looked more intently to see if I could determine our approach as we were making our way to the airport. Then I saw it.

The Lincoln Memorial sat boldly beneath me and the beautiful green grass lining the reflecting pool guided my eyes to the Washington Monument. The Capitol building and the White House were emerging from the fog after an early morning rain. I breathed deeply and thought about my purpose for being here. I knew this visit would provide an opportunity to do what few have had the privilege of doing—to speak to the nation about revival! I imagined the genius of Abraham Lincoln and the log home of his beginning we had just visited a few days prior. I thought of the statue poised elegantly and postured prophetically sitting beneath the canopy of this memorial. I pictured Dr. Martin Luther King, Jr. in 1963 standing on these steps as a national herald of hope and vision. I imagined the power of their voices upon the wind and the influence of their lives delivering a nation. I could hear their voices prophetically shaping future generations and enveloping them in hope. Where are the voices of hope and healing that ride upon the wind in our day? Who will speak today for a people languishing without hope? My mind raced forward trying to imagine the days that lay ahead and the assignment that brought us to this extraordinary city.

I knew upon landing my wife Jennifer and I would get into that hustle and bustle of a busy airport, grab our bags, and solicit a ride on the shuttle to our hotel, so I gave myself permission to take in the greatness of our nation's capital. The fog and the soaking rain were mystical, and the gravity of the assignment lay heavy on my heart. I leaned forward in my seat trying to keep my eye fixed on a small white tent on the ascending steps of the Lincoln Memorial.

I could feel the butterflies in my stomach. I was balancing the feelings of inadequacy with the sheer excitement of being a part of an incredibly historic day. Jennifer and I arrived in the city a couple of days early in order to pray and focus our hearts on the Lord so we might meet Him in a mighty way. Jennifer and I were gathering with many key leaders, pastors, prayer warriors, and all those who bear a burden for the nation. We had been invited to join the Steering Committee for this event over a year earlier by the founders of United Cry DC16, Lewis and Rachel Hogan. The Lord had put an important vision in their hearts; Lewis and Rachel are a couple God is raising up to summon a nation to unity through revival in the local church and through collaboration among pastors and leaders across the country. We are honored to walk with them.

On the drive from the airport to the hotel, I reflected on my beginnings. I grew up in a small town in Eastern Kentucky. In much simpler times my brothers and I would play together and dream big dreams in the big backyard of a tiny white frame house. We would dream of going places beyond the brown grass and bent down fence of that yard, but never could I have imagined that I would stand to speak on the steps of the Lincoln Memorial. However, on this day I found myself entering the nation's capital to stand and deliver a message of hope.

The "Appeal to Heaven" dream has been used to bring great attention to an early flag of our founding fathers, but it was so much more than a night vision depicting a glorious and historic symbol. It was a dream of a coming awakening in the nation, of generational synergy, of prophetic utterance, and of a holy convening for commissioning of the greatest harvest the world has ever seen. The dream has been told and shared by many people who find themselves in the storyline of prophetic anticipation for what God is doing in this nation. The standard has been historically called the "Washington's Cruisers" flag. Its significance is being recovered and its inspiring hope retold all over the world.

United Cry was birthed in Lewis and Rachel's hearts originally, as I have heard them tell it, because God was calling them to fast and pray for unity among leaders. Their hearts burned for revival in the nation, and they were called to build a ministry facilitating synergy among leaders. By the leading of the Holy Spirit through some incredible events, they settled upon April 9, 2016 as the day for a "Joel 2 solemn assembly" when pastors and leaders will lift their voices in a united cry for awakening and revival in the nation.

Sitting in a meeting with the Steering Committee in Dallas, Lewis began to share the historical significance of April 9. These events surrounding April 9 seemed to highlight the incredible prophetic mandate upon the gathering. April 9, 2016 was to be a day of unity among pastors and leaders who were standing as one. On this date in 1865, Robert E. Lee surrendered the last major Confederate army to Ulysses S. Grant at Appomattox Courthouse, bringing an end to the war. Dietrich Bonhoeffer, a German Lutheran pastor, theologian, and anti-Nazi dissident, was executed by hanging on April 9, 1945. The Azusa Street Revival, a historic revival meeting and origin of the Pentecostal movement led by African-American preacher William J. Seymour, began with a meeting on April 9, 1906 and continued until roughly 1915. Finally, Martin Luther King, Jr., civil rights activist, Baptist preacher, and Nobel Peace Prize laureate, was buried on April 9, 1968. He was assassinated by a gunshot wound in Memphis, Tennessee where he had been leading a strike of waste management workers to promote equality and civil rights.

With these historic dates behind us and the gathering now upon us, none of us knew exactly what to expect. What would follow? All we knew to do was to deliberately poise ourselves in humility and cry out with one voice for God to come and quicken the hearts of millions in this nation to seek Him with all our hearts.

Upon landing in Washington, DC, Jennifer and I made our way to the hotel with hearts full of anticipation. We were all keenly aware this was not the only major event happening on this very day to cry out for awakening in the nation. God was orchestrating a national synergy from Washington, DC to Los Angeles. This day would witness two historic gatherings, one on the East Coast and one on the West Coast, both crying out for awakening in the nation. Could this be the beginning of a generational synergy, an unprecedented gathering like the one in my dream?

As we were gathering in Washington, DC, tens of thousands gathered at the Los Angeles Memorial Coliseum in California. This gathering in Los Angeles, *Azusa Now!*, was led by Lou Engle and was very similar in purpose and scope to *United Cry*. The event in Los Angeles had unique components to it, as did the gathering of *United Cry* in Washington, DC, but there was a unity in spirit and in the specific purpose of the two gatherings—America must return to God!

The organizers of these two events worked diligently to see unity and a developing sense of national synergy through two coasts working together. Through video technology the two coasts were linked together in a live broadcast. We were able to connect so that the event in Los Angeles was being played live on giant screens in Washington, DC, and in return *United Cry* was being viewed live in Los Angeles.

Not only were the two coasts connected, but through loyal support for both events millions who resided in between the two coasts could tune in and listen to their radio or television to catch it live. People gathered in homes and churches, watching with great excitement as an unprecedented event unfolded before their eyes and in their hearts. We were also made aware that pastors in other nations were assembled and viewing. One such gathering was shown in Washingto,n DC where pastors had gathered in Jerusalem, Israel, for a *United Cry Jerusalem.*

Washington, DC on April 9, 2016 was bitterly cold. The day gave witness to snow, sleet, rain, and a wind fiercely whipping across the plaza. At one point as I was standing on the stage with Lewis Hogan, the productions manager said, "We are literally moments away from being shut down! If this wind does not cease, the National Park Service will have no other option but to clear the entire area of the people and we are done. You need to get someone out there to pray for this wind to cease!"

Lewis turned to me and said, "Rick, do you want to go do that?" I wasn't sure I wanted to at all! I went to the edge of the platform and, after explaining the situation, asked the people to pray with me that the winds would cease to blow so harshly, or we would have to stop the event. We all believed we had an assignment to fulfill. The production manager told us later he watched as the wind meter began to decrease, and we were able to finish the assignment for the day. Shortly after *United Cry* was over, a harsh wind blew through, knocked down tents, and ruined equipment. It was just that kind of day.

The schedule for the day was focused, simply divided into three major segments—national repentance, national revival, and the Appeal to Heaven and national mobilization of pastors and leaders. I was placed over the revival segment, and in that time slot I was to tell the story of the dream. Prior to the revival segment, ministers would repent to the family of Dr. Martin Luther King, Jr. for not receiving his prophetic vision so eloquently delivered in his "I Have a Dream" speech in 1963 and for not embracing the eradication of division and racism in the nation. Those moments of repentance may very well have been the most powerful time of the entire day. Dr. King's family was gracious, kind, and in every way facilitated the spirit of repentance and reconciliation. True humility was expressed by leaders, and all felt a powerful break-through when it was finished.

The time was fast approaching for me to fulfill my assignment of the day. I was to stand and deliver a mes-sage of hope for America's awakening as I had dreamed it. My feet were soaking wet and felt as if they were frostbitten. My heart was beating rapidly, but I was keenly aware that the Presence of the Lord was hover-ing over that place, and it is the Father's heart to bring in the greatest harvest. I stood and faced the Washington Monument and shivered more at this surreal moment in time than I did from the bitter cold of the day. I began:

> In grave and uncertain times men are called upon to abandon preference and mitigate upon the earth the principles of heaven. These principles are the revealed intentions of a holy God for a wandering and broken humanity. The immutable principles of heav-en are administered by the spirit of prayer in the lives of courageous men and women. It is in these times we live, and it is these prin-ciples we must declare. The spirit of prayer guides us in all humility to boldly bring our appeal for America's greatest awakening be-fore the One who is holy, just, and good.

The subtle embrace of night casts her shadow across the brow of the young maiden of liberty. Night's luring embrace seems to seduce the nation further into an abyss of compromise and chaos. The brilliant hope of the nations and the grand experiment of self-governance seems to be reeling to and fro under the heavy weight of her confusion and toll of her compromise. America is staggering like a drunken fool from compromised values, confusing and unsustainable standards, and a glamorized chaos.

Where is the leadership compelled by a vision for America's future that is truly worthy of her good past? Where are the champions of mercy and the heralds of brotherly love? Where are those who will lay down their lives to bring us together and stand for a cause greater than themselves? Where are they? They are here and they are coming! They are gathered today in Los Angeles crying out for awakening in America! They are gathered everywhere between the East and West coasts today praying and seeking God to come and visit this nation with a quickening resolve of hope and holiness.

Oh, He is coming, my friend! He is coming with an unfurled banner of love for broken humanity in one hand and a flaming torch of the light of His glory and the beauty of His grace in the other.

I awakened in the predawn hours one morning after I had witnessed in a dream an innumerable host gathering. The gathering was of the generations that have gone before us and those who will come after us. They numbered in the thousands! It was amazing. It was a gathering in which each generation heralded with great enthusiasm the generations who followed them.

History is alive with hope evidenced in the past, and nowhere is that hope more evident than standing here on these sacred grounds that we might recall with honor those who have gone before us and yet courageously act on behalf of those who come after. I saw in this dream the nation quickened by God and awakening in the hope of His covenant of promise. These generations gathered in ancient ships, in elegant surreys, in primitive wagons, in early cars sputtering along, in streetcars, and in airplanes, but they came to this meeting, and God met them there.

They came singing and their song bellowed across the strands of the wind and their steps were filled with joyful expectation. They were responding to the invitation of their Lover. Their steps sounded like thunder and their tears like flowing rivers, but the joy of the Lord could be heard in the cadence of their steps and His praise echoed from their mouths like the winds of a mighty storm.

Near the end of the dream I saw hundreds, maybe thousands of ministers representing every generation gather together in unity on a massive platform for the commissioning of America's greatest awakening. Oh, how they were one! Then I saw in the hands of a dear minister friend of mine a flag being waved—a flag I had never seen before. Upon telling my wife, Jennifer, the dream the next morning, she encouraged me to Google the flag and see if it was a real flag. Much to our amazement it was the Washington's Cruisers flag from 1775. I had never seen the flag before. It is a white flag with a centered evergreen tree and the words "Appeal to Heaven" as a brilliant banner above the tree. This is not my flag!

This is America's flag left for us by the founding fathers to remind a future generation of the words of John Locke in 1690—that when a nation or a people no longer have a just recourse for help and intervention, it is time to make an appeal to heaven, declaring America's best days lie before her and not behind her. Like God did in the days of old, He is luring America into the wilderness that He might speak tenderly to her, restoring her, renewing her, and reviving her! In the "Appeal to Heaven" dream there was a single chair placed on the edge of this massive platform and I was asked a question: "Are you ready to take your place?" It was not a question for me alone, but for each of us, I think. This question continues to demand a response.

I believe America is hungry for revival! I believe America is ripe for revival! The winds of the Spirit are about to blow across the land and ignite the hearts of millions with His revelation. I believe that today marks the beginning of fresh, new days. "I revealed myself to those who did not ask for me; I was found by those who did not seek me. To a nation that did not call on my name, I said, *'Here am I, here am I'*" (Isa. 65:1 NIV).

There are moments in time, though rare, when we can witness with our own eyes and glean from our own understanding that something unusual is at hand. The rare moments in time when a convergence of two paths brings us to focus on one great hope. It is the certainty of hope that God has neither abandoned us nor does He have any intention of doing so. "We have this hope as an anchor for the soul, firm and secure" (Heb. 6:19 NIV). Rather, God is calling this nation to come before Him in humility, desire, and encounter Him afresh in the fiery baptism of His love and grace. *"If my people who are called by my name humble themselves, and pray and seek my face and turn from their wicked ways, then I will hear from heaven and will forgive their sin and heal their land"* (2 Chron. 7:14 ESV). He is calling the nation to recklessly abandon ourselves at the feet of His cross and encounter Him!

My small contribution was over in a few brief moments, but this was but one step in the remarkable journey that brought us to this place. Together we must explore the prophetic utterances of the dream, the remarkable people we have met along the way, and some of the most incredible encounters one could possibly imagine.

Chapter 3

An Angel of Strategy

Though [the vision] *tarry, wait for it; because it will surely come, it will not tarry* (Habakkuk 2:3 KJV).

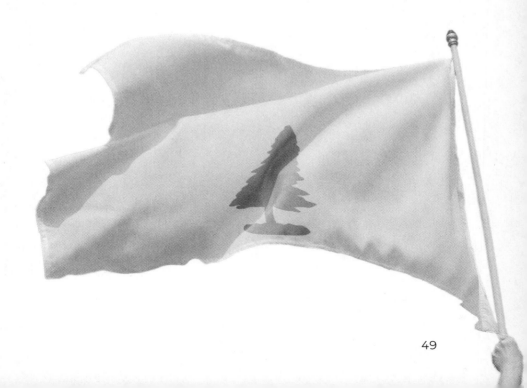

The long night that precedes America's brilliant dawn will be filled with visions and dreams that mark the path, chart the course, and release divine strategy for the greatest awakening. An encounter with the Lord is like a shadow upon the ground as it fades quickly, shifts continually, and yet when intentionally stewarded can bring unimaginable revelation and insight. Such encounters can be carried for years and truly alter the course of a life.

I had a dramatic vision of an angel while in Argentina a few years ago. I have spoken of it publicly only a few times and have not written about it until now. The reason, I trust, will be clear by the end of this chapter. I knew that encounter marked the beginning of a unique journey.

Before I embarked on an international flight to Argentina, Jennifer handed me a new journal while giving me very specific instructions. "Ricky, this trip will change your life. I feel strongly that you must journal, and watch for Tuesday, because Tuesday is a big day! The Lord wanted me to tell you to watch, see, and record what He shows you!" I knew she had heard from the Lord, so I tucked the journal into my backpack and flew out for Argentina. I had no idea all that would unfold in the days that lay ahead.

I was going to Argentina for a conference at the King of Kings Church with Claudio and Betty Freidzon, Sergio Scataglini, and Carlos Annacondia. My travel itinerary included an early arrival that I might attend a Carlos Annacondia crusade for a couple of nights outside Buenos Aires. I was tremendously excited to attend this crusade as Argentina had been marked by the power of a sweeping national revival.

When the conference began, the leadership announced the schedule for the week: "Don't forget Tuesday morning is ladies' morning!" As I contemplated whether I should attend the Tuesday morning gathering, I continued to remember what Jennifer had said about the upcoming Tuesday. I went to the Tuesday morning meeting rather reluctantly, but it was here the Lord began to unfold a series of encounters and revelations that would radically shift my life.

The Angel of Strategy for Awakening and Kingdom Advancement

The minister that morning was ministering powerfully while sharing the story of the early days of the Argentine revival. She spoke specifically about the *anointing of one*—a necessary increase in the anointing of the Holy Spirit to allow ministers and their spouses to work together in greater unity and to function more powerfully in the Kingdom together as one. Near the end of her teaching, she had the congregation stand. As we stood up, I saw before me on the platform a vision of a towering angel. The angel was brilliant to look upon with magnificent white hair and wielding a sword being held with both hands. The sword was elevated with the tip to the ceiling shielding the face of the angel. When I looked upon the angel, I saw coming out of the two-edged blades of the sword the flags of the nations. The flags made a complete circle. I immediately began to pray, and I felt the angel that I was looking upon was the "Angel of Strategy for Awakening and Kingdom Advancement."

I had never had such a vision as that. I quickly pulled my journal out and wrote down exactly what I had seen and heard. Further, I knew there was a far greater significance to what had just unfolded before my eyes than simply a vision. I felt the Lord was ministering to me concerning the coming awakening among the nations. I felt the Lord was releasing strategy upon the earth and that we would see revival and an awakening that would sweep millions into the Kingdom around the world. The minister gave an altar call and I rushed forward to respond in prayer. The atmosphere of the meeting seemed electric, and I was in awe of the vision of the angel. I had no idea what was happening in the world at that very moment.

After being ministered to at the altar I found a place to lie on the ground at the front of the church and try to soak in all that I had seen and heard that morning. As I lay on the floor, the man who had accompanied me on this trip knelt beside me and said, "We are under attack!" I thought, *Please, not now! I am praying!* He insisted on interrupting me and proceeded to tell me the United States was under a major terrorist attack. He told me the twin towers had been flown into by airplanes, and the Pentagon and other major facilities had been attacked as well. In addition, the United States military was shooting passenger airliners out of the sky as they knew more planes had been hijacked with plans of terrorists flying into major facilities of national significance. Obviously, not all the initial reports that we received were completely accurate, but this day was Tuesday, September 11, 2001.

The conclusion of that service was marked by the minister who had preached that morning admonishing the crowd to "mark your Bibles on where you were the day the world changed." We met with fellow conventioneers from the United States to pray and encourage one another. We were told it could be thirty days before we could catch a flight to return home as all flights had been grounded and cellular communication was not available either. What could all of this possibly mean? What do you do when the Lord ushers you into a moment of revelation that seems overwhelming and unfolding in real time?

We carried this encounter in our hearts and, sure enough, in a few days we were able to return home more convinced than ever God was doing amazing things. I cannot overstate the value of faithfully recording dreams and visions, because sometimes it is years before the fruit of such encounters become visible. Upon returning home I sought to diligently record the significance of the times in which we were living and to process the messages the Lord was ministering through this remarkable vision. It is clear today that the Lord is releasing a strategy for the advancement of His Kingdom upon the earth through awakening and transforming revival.

One of the things we have implemented through this vision and encounter in Argentina is what we have called an "Awakening Mosaic." We are completely convinced the awakening at hand will be not personality driven but will be centered around the manifest Presence of God in the hearts and lives of ordinary, everyday men and women. This Awakening Mosaic is a beautiful expression of the diversity of Kingdom leadership coming together upon the three pillars of awakening—humility, honor, and holiness or the Heart of the Father for a generational move of God. We will discuss this more in Chapter 9.

Why do visions come? Why do such encounters occur and how should we process those glimpses of revelation the Lord provides for us? How do we steward that which the Holy Spirit has entrusted to us through visions and dreams?

One such encounter worthy of mentioning happened on an ordinary Wednesday night at the conclusion of a worship gathering. I was standing near the front of the church, and I glanced up out of the corner of my eye and saw a middle-aged man entering the rear of the sanctuary. Upon entering he inquired, "Is Poppa in the house? Is Poppa and Momma in the house?" I was a little surprised but welcomed the man into our gathering. He told me he had come from Africa and was sent by God to bring "Poppa and Momma" a message. I asked a few of our elders to gather around us so that they too may hear this word of the Lord. The man proceeded to give me one of the most accurate and alarming words of our entire ministry.

He began by saying he had never been to Florida before, and that he had flown into Texas just a few days earlier. He continued by saying he had been in Pensacola, Florida, for three days inquiring of the Lord where he might find "Poppa and Momma." The minister went on to say that he had parked in front of churches all over the city and inquired of the Lord, but it was not until he parked in front of our church that he felt the confirmation to come inside and inquire about "Poppa and Momma."

He released the word in a way I cannot completely recall. I am deeply saddened by this, but he began by saying that God had shown me in a dream that awakening was coming to the nations. He said the Lord had shown us through unusual encounters and dreams His plans for a mighty revival and harvest of souls. He went on to describe the dream and declare the awakening would be greater in scope than the Azusa Street revival, and God would shake nations. However, as he continued to speak he ministered to my wife and me as if he were living in our home and told us of things that must happen before we would see the fullness of this move of God. He gave us insight into the days ahead and instruction on what must yet transpire.

We were able to extend our visit with this minister into the next day. When we met for lunch the following day, he continued to release amazing words of hope and visions of what would come. He also told us that to prove his words were from God someone was going to give me a new truck. Further, he said the truck given to us would be like the one given to him—a white, four-door Toyota truck with tan leather interior. I was unclear as to the best response to that, so I simply asked, "Would you remind the Lord that I am a Ford man?" We laughed, and he said it's easy. Within a very few days the ministry was gifted a beautiful white Ford F-150 with four doors and tan leather interior. The amazing couple who donated the truck had no knowledge of the word that had been given to us at all. The incredible encounters such as this one have continued to happen over the course of the last few years.

The journey of faith along the trail of fire in the hope of awakening and transforming revival is seldom dull when we learn to walk in and navigate our lives by the leading of the Holy Spirit.

Stewarding Visions and Dreams

I want to introduce a few keys that will provide insight into how we steward such encounters, but first let's be clear on the understanding of the word *steward*. The definition of *steward* according to *Merriam-Webster* is "one employed or tasked to manage domestic concerns; one appointed to supervise the provision and distribution in an institution; one who actively directs affairs." It is essential we learn to steward a vision or dream until the next step becomes very clear for us to take. Here are a few important keys to unlocking the power of your encounters with the Lord:

1. Avoid Isolation!

We must steward visions and dreams by constantly giving ourselves permission to see the bigger picture unfolding in the Spirit. Generally, the Lord is not going to share the entire scope of the vision or dream.

Invariably there will be events that both precede and follow the encounter. We must learn to see the big picture and steward well by not letting a single encounter become the entire story.

2. Allow Involvement!

We must understand that usually others are involved in some way with the encounter either directly or indirectly. In this angelic encounter and the events that followed, there were numerous people involved to either position me or prepare me in ways they could not have known. My wife, Jennifer, gave me the journal before departing the United States on our initial flight. I had never journaled before, but I have faithfully ever since. She gave me a word to "watch out for Tuesday—something big is going to happen." Without that word I may have missed that morning session because it was advertised as a "women's meeting," and I was unclear whether men were to attend. Our journey will always include interaction with others who often unknowingly are used by the Lord to help prepare us or position us for a wonderful encounter. We learn to steward visions and dreams by allowing others to have access to our journey.

3. Always Journal!

It cannot be overstated that one of the most significant keys to stewarding visions and dreams is to be firmly committed to journaling your own encounters. When we record the unfolding of visions and dreams at the time of the encounter, the accuracy is preserved, and a path begins to form that becomes easy to follow as you move on to the discovery of this and other encounters that lay ahead.

4. Avoid Exposure!

One of the keys to stewarding visions and dreams is to avoid the natural tendency to want to share the vision or dream too soon or even with the wrong people. We can prematurely and unnecessarily expose the vision or dream to harsh criticism and scrutiny, causing us to become doubtful about its validity. I will often encourage people to not share a vision or dream at all until it has been accurately recorded without the influence of others.

5. Ask Questions!

Do not be afraid as you pray and seek to process the vision or dream. The questions that you ask yourself, bring before the Lord in your prayer time. I have found it very beneficial to ask questions of those around me so that I might learn what *they* were sensing from the Lord at the time of the encounter.

Though the vision tarry, wait for it, because it will surely come—it will not tarry (see Hab. 2:3 KJV). God is the giver of visions. When God gives a vision, ours is to obey and enter into that vision. God will bring it to pass in His time and His way.

Chapter 4

Awaken the Brokenhearted Ones

The Lord is near to the brokenhearted and saves those who are crushed in spirit (Psalm 34:18).

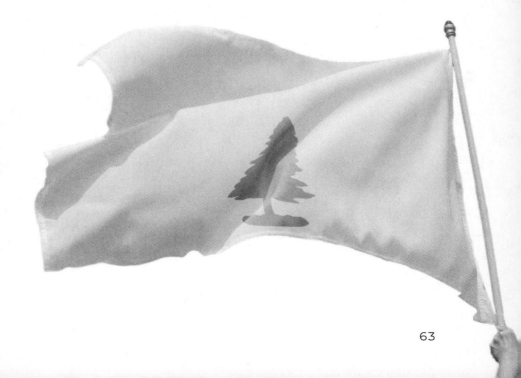

I sat quietly in the nearly empty auditorium. Suddenly, I felt the Holy Spirit drawing me aside to come with Him and pray. I went to the front of the room and simply lay on the floor and began to pray. The Holy Spirit opened the eyes of my heart that I might see through a vision the awakening and healing of the brokenhearted ones.

The Vision

A man was standing at the center of a prayer circle with a heart in his left hand. He was holding the heart up in the air, boldly displayed for all to see. In his right hand he was holding a long knife with the tip of the blade resting against the heart but doing no damage. The people in the circle were aware of the most unusual position of the heart, but all were silent. No one seemed alarmed or concerned about it at all, nor were they concerned for the knife pointed and positioned to do utter destruction. They seemed to simply be praying.

I began to inquire of the Lord, "Whose heart is this? Why is there no concern for it?" I knew the Lord was ministering to me that the heart was mine. Through this vision the Lord revealed that not only was He doing a deep work in me, but He was also about to move mightily in the lives of the brokenhearted ones. The Lord immediately ministered to me two incredible things. First, He was about to awaken and restore the brokenhearted ones. He ministered to me that a key to unlocking transforming revival in the Church and awakening in the nation is the anointing to heal the brokenhearted. Second, the heart belonged to me and He had come to heal my brokenness and give me the courage to take back my heart.

A broken heart can be found anywhere. A broken heart is no "respecter of persons," and multitudes carry silently in their lives a heart broken by abusers or even by dear friends. Millions suffer silently with a broken heart, but the Lord is releasing a fresh anointing to heal and restore them.

Can you imagine the revival that would manifest if God began to move mightily in the lives of those whose broken hearts have up to this moment paralyzed them? I believe the Lord is about to sweep through congregations, fellowships, and homes breaking the bonds of despair and bringing restored hope and healing to hearts and relationships.

In the vision I stepped into the center of a circle of people, and I looked at the man with the heart in his hand and said, "I have come to make an announcement. I have come to take my heart back! I love each of you.

I forgive you. I release you. I am moving on, and I have come to take my heart with me." When the broken heart is healed, hope returns and transformation occurs.

Consider the years that lay behind Joseph in Genesis 45:1-11 and the remarkable healing in the life of his family. When we read this passage of Scripture, we are literally jumping right into the middle of one of the most astonishing stories in all the Bible. As we consider this passage, we find Joseph about to reveal himself to his brothers from whom he had been separated for years after they sold him into slavery. Joseph has known privilege as a favored son and brokenness as a forgotten slave. The events unfolding in this passage of Scripture are dramatic and life changing, but oh, how they quicken our hearts to believe.

We are in a season wherein we will witness the bold unlocking of God's purposes and plans in the earth. It is time for the transformation of our lives and homes through the awakening of a broken heart. A broken heart encounters God's love and healing and is filled with hope.

Consider three keys to awakening the brokenhearted ones. We are going to look at these principles from history and the Bible, particularly in the life of Joseph.

1. *Understanding Your Place!*

In Genesis 37 we find Joseph confident of his future because he had a clear understanding that the favor of his father rested upon him. He was confident in the blessing of his father. We are in the days of the revelation of the Father's heart! I heard that clearly on a Sunday morning that launched a revival lasting for an entire year!

It was a Sunday morning in March. The Holy Spirit had ministered to me about four months earlier to watch the season of Passover, because He was going to move mightily among us. We spent thousands of dollars to prepare the church through cleaning, painting, and sprucing things up in the anticipation of a mighty revival and outpouring of God. The entire congregation was moving in expectation for the visitation. Suddenly, on a Sunday morning in March as I was standing to the right side of the pulpit and sharing about what God was doing in Kentucky, I had my very first open vision ever. It was as though I saw the Lord walk into the room, and in His right hand He was holding a burning torch, and in His left was an unfurled banner. I nearly lost my breath. As He made His way toward me, I thought I was dying and possibly this was my life passing before my eyes. As He came closer, I felt as if He was washing my face with the fire in His hand, and I ended up on the floor at approximately 11:15 AM before my entire congregation. It would be right at 2:30 PM before I would be able to pick myself up off the floor.

In the encounter I felt as if the Holy Spirit ministered some very important details. I heard deeply in my spirit,

"There is a move of God coming that no building will contain, and no ministry will control!" Second, I heard the Holy Spirit minister to me three foundation pillars of this great awakening—humility, honor, and holiness. I believe we will see purity and power remarry in the season of this awakening. We must contend for renewed humility in the hearts of the believers, and we must learn once again to honor and prefer others better than ourselves.

So how do we understand our place? We begin with a return to the fundamental reality that we need each other desperately and no one person or ministry will carry the full revelation of the events unfolding. Also, we will see many streams and expressions of worship, evangelism, and discipleship during this awakening. "The fear of the Lord is the instruction for wisdom, and before honor comes humility" (Prov. 15:33). Second, we take our place by developing a lifestyle of honoring others. "Glory and honour are in his presence; strength and gladness are in his place" (1 Chron. 16:27 KJV). Third, we must pursue once again the fire of His holiness cleansing, sanctifying, and in every way equipping and empowering the believer for service and life. "Who is like unto thee, O Lord, among the gods? who is like thee, glorious in holiness, fearful in praises, doing wonders?" (Exod. 15:11 KJV).

We must allow faith to rise within us and bring confidence in the Father's purpose for our lives and His power to bring to pass what He has promised. You can be confident for your future because the Father has a purpose for you and me during this time. Celebrate the blessing of the Lord that is being poured out now upon us and increasing the anointing of His Holy Spirit.

2. *Unveiling Your Hope!*

Even though Joseph was betrayed by his brothers, he went on to declare that it was God's plan that he might be sent ahead to secure the future of his family during a devastating famine. In their betrayal of Joseph, he went before them to secure their future! In Genesis 42, Joseph revealed the deep pain of his brothers' betrayal, but in chapters 43 and 44 he revealed the problem of the brothers' hearts. They were jealous of Joseph and coveted Joseph's relationship with his father. The brothers had carried for years the hidden secret pain of what they had done to Joseph, but now Joseph was about to expose that pain to unlock their future for them!

WHEN PAIN IS EXPOSED, IT IS A SURE SIGN OF A PROMISE UNVEILED!

Make no mistake about it, there is unmeasurable trauma that feels intensely personal under the weight of a broken heart. But God knows how to resolve the conflict, release through forgiveness, and restore the brokenhearted ones to great freedom and blessing.

3. Unlocking Your Future!

In the encounter I explained at the beginning of this chapter when I saw my heart in the hands of another person, I was compelled to make the declaration to all who were standing in that circle that I had come to take my heart back. I was taking back my future. I was resolving past conflict and allowing the Lord to come and heal the places in my life that felt shattered by my own choices or by the decisions of others. In great moves of God, there is revelation given concerning the fear of the Lord and the power of forgiveness. A key to healing the brokenhearted ones lies within the promise of radical and wild forgiveness.

We were in revival in Lenoir City, Tennessee, and I was seated on a mop bucket hiding in a church janitors' closet. I was longing to quit the ministry much too early simply because of a broken heart. I did not know what to do. I did not know if I needed healing, forgiveness, or deliverance. I just knew I could not continue with a conflicted and broken heart. I had reverberating in my head principles I had been taught all my life. The principle was this: "We are to forgive and forget!" The problem was, with the scope of my issues that I could not control from when I was a child, I could not forget and did not know how to forgive because I knew I could not forget. I knew something had to change. It was not my future that needed to be unlocked, but it was me who needed to be unlocked. If God could unlock me from the trauma of a broken heart, He could unfold my future before me easily.

Seated on the mop bucket, the Holy Spirit guided me to truths in Matthew 18 that would forever change my life. The Lord ministered that passage to me from a message entitled "How to Forgive When You Cannot Forget." It was simple then, but life-transforming still. That day He taught me the principles of forgiveness:

1. Forgiveness creates the deepest awareness of sin! Forgiveness never demands I forget the offense or justify the deeds of the offender. Forgiveness never demands I skirt around the issue or bury my head in the sand. Forgiveness releases the power of grace to look full into the face of the offender and still choose to forgive, to release, and to move on boldly into a future made free with a heart that has been healed.

2. Forgiveness costs the innocent one! This was difficult for me. I think it might be human nature to desire the guilty pay a great price and the innocent go free, but

in the cross of Jesus I was boldly reminded that it was He, the Innocent One, who
paid the price for my forgiveness. I realized while seated on that bucket that the
offender had passed years earlier, and if
my freedom demanded his willingness to
make this right I could simply never be
free or forgiven. I learned there my forgiveness never requires an action from
another person, it never demands permission from the offender to move on,
and it never hinges on their willingness
to "make it right." I could simply understand in Jesus I have been forgiven, and in
Him *alone* I can forgive others and move
on.

3. Forgiveness conditions one to forgive on
   the basis that I have been forgiven.

*Peter came up and said to him, "Lord, how
often will my brother sin against me, and I
forgive him? As many as seven times?" Jesus
said to him, "I do not say to you seven times,
but until seventy-seven times"* (Matthew
18:21-22 ESV).

With this promise of hope and power of the Holy
Spirit, I wept that day sitting on a mop bucket and

allowed the Lord to begin the amazing work of grace to heal the broken heart.

The Anointing

Jesus entered the synagogue and read from Isaiah 61 one of the most remarkable prophecies in the Old Testament:

> *The Spirit of the Lord is upon me, because he hath anointed me to preach the gospel to the poor; he hath sent me to heal the broken-hearted, to preach deliverance to the captives, and recovering of sight to the blind, to set at liberty them that are bruised* (Luke 4:18 KJV).

Among many other significant truths, we find in this passage the purpose of the anointing.

As I have written these words, I have prayed for all of those who read this who may be suffering from a broken heart. Jesus came to heal the brokenhearted ones. The word for *heal* in this verse literally means "to cure, to heal, and to make whole" (Strong's G2390). Also, in this verse the word for *brokenhearted* means "bruised, broken in pieces, broken in shivers, shattered" (Strong's G4937). God's mercy and love will make their hearts whole again and restore their hope.

The Application

1. Allow the Lord to heal you of the paralysis caused by a broken heart! Seek the heart of the Father and let mercy flow through you to forgive and release those who have so mishandled your heart. Your deliverance and healing never depend on someone else's decision.

2. Allow the Lord to restore the passionate pursuit of your dream! The Word of the Lord is for you and His promises are yes and amen! The Lord is giving to you dreams that will direct you to your destiny. Pursue the Lord again and forgive those who have hurt you. Through the power of mercy and the strength of grace to move forward, you can forgive others and move into your greatest days. You do not need someone else's permission to enjoy the freedom forgiveness brings.

3. Allow the Lord to bring personal revival to the place of your brokenness. The Lord has come to fully restore and heal, and the purpose of the anointing is to fulfill to a measure of fullness the promises that are found in Jesus!

Awakening is coming to the nations of the earth, and it may very well begin in the simple places where the Lord manifests His anointing to heal the brokenhearted ones. It is time to take your heart back and move into all that God has for you.

Chapter 5

The Spirit of Prayer

In grave and uncertain times, men are called upon to abandon preference and bring to earth the principles of heaven. These are principles God has revealed for a wandering and broken humanity. These immutable principles of heaven are administered by the spirit of prayer in the lives of courageous men and women. It is in these times we live, and it is these principles we must decree. Prayer requires humility to bring our appeal before the One who is holy, just, and good. We have no other recourse and no greater appeal than to the One who has promised to respond. John Locke wrote in the *Second Treatise of Government* that those "who having no appeal on earth to right them [no ability to correct what is wrong or unjust], they are left to the only remedy in such cases, *an appeal to heaven.*"[1] It is time for America to make her appeal to heaven; it is time to return to prayer.

When I awakened after having the dream of the Appeal to Heaven flag and America's great awakening, I sat silently in my home and contemplated not the symbols in the dream, but the sound that was released in the dream. What sound would be released in the earth if leaders began to come together for a cause greater than any one of us individually? What would it sound like if generations began to labor together in a spirit of honor and humility? The sound that I heard was the most stunning and incredible part of the entire dream. The dream marked my life with the hope of seeing the sound of awakening released in the land.

What are you hearing today? Would you describe what you are hearing as a requiem or a reformation? Let's consider this question and its challenges.

What lay ahead for the nations—a political requiem or a spiritual reformation? A requiem is a mass for the dead, a solemn chant such as a dirge. It is a lament of mourning of great darkness that demands no repentance or vision. It is the last chord of a solemn farewell to something held most valuable or someone once held very dear and precious. It is the scorn of hopelessness that whips across the barren landscape of a broken and confused generation. Political requiem is despair bound in the chains of complete helplessness, and very tragically there are many people who, upon viewing the manifest condition of culture and the acceptable values of society, feel isolated and hopeless. They live with fear as the fruit of what they consume, but there is a greater reality. A much greater reality!

The sound of awakening is the dawn of hope and the sunrise of faith in the lives of everyday men and women.

The sound of awakening will be dramatic, piercing the darkness and illuminating the shadows of despair and hopelessness. The sound of awakening is the echo of a transformed heart multiplied many times over. I propose to you that we might consider together that it is way too early for a funeral dirge of faith in the earth, and in fact, we may very well be at the beginning of another wonderful spiritual awakening. The sound of awakening can be heard in the land.

Part of prayer for this time includes stewarding the revelation the Lord gives to us through His Holy Bible and the Holy Spirit, including dreams, visions, and prophetic words.

The Lincoln Memorial and the "Appeal to Heaven" Dream

I remember the opportunity to stand on the steps of the Lincoln Memorial at the edge of the National Mall on a blistering cold day in April and share the story of my dream of America's Greatest Awakening and the Appeal to Heaven flag. It was as if I could hear hope resonating throughout the Washington Mall as we reflected upon the dream of awakening in the land. I could hear the rhetorical speeches, prayer gatherings, and songs of worship colliding in the atmosphere over us. I stood with the incredible statue of Abraham Lincoln behind me, and I reflected about his days.

The unprecedented times in which Abraham Lincoln lived demanded an exceptional leader. Still today, many presidents who have followed in his *path of humility* have longed to learn the way of his steps. What grace was upon him that enabled him to lead without fear and love without guile? Was it the humble beginnings on this wilderness frontier? Was it listening when his mother read the Bible and he noticed a glistening in her eyes? Was it because on Knob Creek in the Kentucky wilderness he saw slaves traveling down the old Cumberland Road to be sold? Was it his relationship with Peter Cartwright, John Quincy Adams, or a host of other powerful contemporaries who provoked a sense of great purpose and destiny in his life? Through humility Abraham Lincoln learned to abandon preference and bring the principles of heaven to earth as president of the United States. He would become known as "the great emancipator." In the words of Andrew Murry, "Let our one desire and our fervent prayer be, to be humbled with Him and like Him; let us accept gladly whatever can humble us before God or men;—this alone is the path to the glory of God."[2]

Where are those who will abandon their biases and administer the immutable principles of heaven upon the earth today? A people will fall when our remedy is violence and our words are vitriolic. We must return to a place of humility and yield to the Holy Spirit to produce heavenly results. It was Lincoln who declared:

> And whereas it is the duty of nations as well as of men, to own their dependence upon the overruling power of God, to confess their sins and transgressions, in humble sorrow, yet with assured hope that genuine repentance will lead to mercy and pardon; and to recognize the sublime truth, announced in the Holy Scriptures and proven by all history, that those nations only are blessed whose God is the Lord.[3]

There are always outstanding leaders who emerge in times of great revival and awakening. Let's not limit the leaders who are powerful to those prominent ones positioned on the platform. There are those upon whom the Lord pours out the spirit of supplication (see Zech. 12:10). To these leaders their sound resonates off the walls of an inner closet as they travail before the Lord. To these notable leaders all things are subordinate to prayer and intercession. They have surrendered hearts and live subjugated lives under the flow of God's revelation in the posture of prayer. They, like Jesus, leave the multitudes wondering as they walk away into a glorious garden of prayer.

God Reveals His Father's Heart When We Pray

Praying aligns us with the heart of the Father and restores us in love. The Father heart of God is most splendidly revealed through the cross of Jesus and the power of His resurrection, ascension, and gift of the Holy Spirit. Our Lord has responded to the darkest depths of man's depravity with the glorious hope of His love. His unfailing love will cause us to redefine our priorities, our purpose, and the strategy of our mission. Jesus never preached on healing or deliverance, but His love manifested both of these throughout His ministry. His immutable principles of the Kingdom are the invisible truths that transform the visible reality of brokenness and sin in the earth. We were sent to manifest the reign of the King upon the earth, and such a task demands prayer that brings revelation of the Father's heart.

The Spirit of Prayer Restores Humility

When a nation seems to be reeling on the brink of chaos with political voices screaming and the voices of the pulpit silent, it's time for the wilderness leaders to arise in humility and pray without ceasing. *It is in this posture of humility the Lord embraces a nation and leads her into holiness.* So many incredible things are happening all over the nation and there is a sound of awakening in the air. America's hope is not only discovered in the latest prophetic decree, it is renewed in the place of humility and prayer. The spirit of prayer that will once again posture the Church (Ekklesia) in humility is America's hope. The Bible says, "I will break the pride of your power; and I will make your heaven as iron, and your earth as brass" (Lev. 26:19 KJV). This is a powerful truth consistent with the biblical understanding of pride throughout Scripture. The word for *pride* in this verse means, among other things, arrogance and self-exaltation. It is the spirit of prayer that breaks the power of self-aggrandizing pride that foolishly exalts itself above God and others.

I remember hearing a powerful minister years ago ask a stunning question, "Will America return to God through desperation or through revelation?" Oh, that it might be by revelation! Let the spirit of prayer grip our hearts that every barrier seeking to divide us will be consumed upon the altar of intercession, and every high thing that hinders would be brought down. A generation is emerging in the land—a generation no longer willing to tolerate the indifference of the past and who together are standing to make a united cry for America's awakening and transforming revival. The Lord will soon come and heal the land through the greatest awakening the nation has ever seen.

The united cry comes when each individual seeks the face of God. That's when we are all unified—facing the same direction, looking at the same person, hearing the same voice. Awakening starts with each individual. Second Chronicles 7:14 is a command with a promise:

If my people, which are called by my name, shall humble themselves, and pray, and seek my face, and turn from their wicked ways; then will I hear from heaven, and will forgive their sin, and will heal their land (KJV).

God is very clear about what we must do and what He will do. God's name is His nature and His nature is mercy. Through His mercy, God has called us out of bondage. We must humble ourselves. In other words, we must confess our sinful ways are wrong and turn away from them. We must seek His face. What does that mean? It means we must talk to Him, not just about Him; sing to Him, not just sing about Him. We must focus on Him and listen to Him, pray and seek His face in a quiet place away from the crowds just like when Jesus went away from the crowds to a quiet place to pray. The healing starts with each individual, you and me, living in the light of Christ, humbling and turning away, focusing, and praying. God is calling this generation to confess our idolatry and look for Him. He will heal our land, our nation, because He is merciful and because His purpose to do so originated in Him. He

Himself is zealous to do this! (See Isaiah 9:6.) Will you join in a spirit of prayer to pray in unity that God will awaken our nations and heal our land?

The Spirit of Prayer Renews Hope

The underlying principle we continue to seek to emphasize is that we have a responsibility to respond correctly and properly steward our dreams and visions. While ministering, I will often remark that "anything can happen in a dream," and it is true. It is true not just within the framework of the dream itself but through the practical application and stewardship of a dream or vision. Dreams and visions of the Lord can often produce great hope! I have been enormously encouraged many times through dreams and visions, but it really gets exciting when someone takes the dream and begins to practically implement some expression of it, releasing the hope contained within it. I remember hearing Chuck Pierce say once, "When God enters time and speaks to you, faith enters your atmosphere and fear must flee."

Hope, born in the inspiring revelation of God, helps us abandon fear and release faith. Remember how God used a plague to liberate His people and press them into His promise? He demonstrated His power over the sun, Egypt's greatest symbol of worship. Pharaoh was worshiped as the resurrection of the sun god Rah. God demonstrated His power over both through the plague of darkness. This plague revealed the Lord Himself as the Greater Light; those who trust in Him find freedom, faith, and security and move into His promises.

The future is always linked with hope! Someone once described hope as a cord you can grab a hold of, pulling yourself into an expected and blessed outcome. Hope produces expectation, and expectation allows us the grace to respond correctly and come into the fullness of our best future.

Requiem or Reformation?

A generation is emerging determined to move forward. Their hearts are burning with the brilliance of His manifest glory, and they are releasing a sound of hope in the earth. We must learn to see the invisible that we might achieve the impossible! Outpourings of glory are often preceded by the power from prayer and intercession. What are you envisioning for America's future?

Notes

1. John Locke, Second Treatise of Government, "Chapter III: Of the State of War," Section 20 (1690), Project Gutenberg ebook, July 28, 2010, https://www.gutenberg.org/files/7370/7370-h/7370-h.htm.

2. Andrew Murry, *Humility: The Beauty of Holiness* (Los Angeles, CA: Indo-European Publishing, 2009), 61.

3. Abraham Lincoln, "Proclamation Appointing a National Fast Day," March 30, 1863, Abraham Lincoln Online, Speeches and Writings, http://www.abrahamlincolnonline.org/lincoln/speeches/fast.htm.

Chapter 6

Seven Generations: The Convergence and the Commissioning

It will come about after this that I will pour out My Spirit on all mankind; and your sons and daughters will prophesy, your old men will dream dreams, your young men will see visions (Joel 2:28).

In the "Appeal to Heaven" dream, I saw seven generations coming together in a remarkable way. This was one of the most powerful moments in the dream. In an incredible show of overwhelming support for one another, each generation would wildly dance and applaud the arrival of the generation after them. In addition, each of the generations, upon arriving, would be singing and worshiping in their unique style for the time in which they lived. There was no combative spirit against one another. The worship of each generation blended with generations before and after even though their styles and sounds were dramatically different from one another. This dramatically different style would beautifully blend and build in a synergistic release. With the compounding of voices came the compounding of excitement and power!

I realized the dream showed a generational convergence of worship along with a grand commissioning for the reaping of an end-time global harvest. What we are witnessing today is a convergence of generations and the empowering of a commission to carry the revelation of awakening in the nations on the earth today. Things will most assuredly look different in many ways moving into the future, but make no mistake, the Holy Spirit is pouring out upon generations and is equipping, enlisting, and empowering ordinary men and women to not just encounter Him but to be His glory. The Lord is ministering this to a myriad of people, and it may not look or sound like we might think it should, but at the end of the day, it is all about Jesus and His glory being poured out upon the earth, winning a mighty harvest of souls. Our response to His revelation catapults us into profound mobilization against all chaos.

At the end of the "Appeal to Heaven" dream, I saw the gentlemanly man who had escorted me through the dream step to the podium and invite the generations to come forward and receive a commissioning of the Holy Spirit for the coming global harvest. It was a stunning sight to see each of the generations come forward to receive the blessing of all those generations who had gone before with all those who will come after. The word I heard in the dream was that there is a move of God coming that will include the synergy of the ages. Each generation is connected to the previous as the unfolding plan of God moves mightily through the hearts and lives of people in each generation. Also, each generation prepares the way for the generations to come. Our generation is no exception, and as the days of man unfold in the drama of God's history, we will discover afresh the blessing of God that rests on each generation.

I was flying into Washington, DC to meet with key prayer leaders and a group of transformational partners from around the world contending for awakening and revival in the nations. Typically when I fly, I choose to be out on the earliest flight possible, even if this means that I must wait an extended period of time. This time I arrived nearly three hours before the others. I sat alone in the upper level of the airport. I was seated in a coffee shop working on my computer and drinking a cup of coffee very casually. Suddenly I had a man tap me on the shoulder, and as I turned to look at him, I recognized him immediately to be a local police officer in full uniform. He asked if I would mind stepping outside to speak with him a minute. I obliged, of course. Upon stepping outside the coffee shop, he asked me if I would mind going down one level with him. Again, greatly intrigued, I went with him without hesitation.

As we were going to the lower level, I asked him if there was a problem. He assured me there was not, and they simply were having a news conference downstairs and had a piece of equipment he thought I might be willing to help him move. *You have got to be kidding me!* We got to the lower level and, sure enough, there was a golf-cart-type vehicle we politely pushed out of the camera shot. He thanked me and walked off, leaving me there alone! I decided to stay for the news conference and see what was up.

I secured a nondescript place leaning against the wall and simply was watching news cameras, still photographers, and other interesting news people milling about waiting for the arrival of their guest. *Who might this be?* Suddenly, I saw a small entourage of people making their way toward the microphone with a Catholic priest and an archbishop I recognized from national news stations.

The distinguished-looking man stepped to the microphone. All the reporters were clamoring and cameras were flashing, but he politely stopped them and said before taking questions that he had some business to take care of from the Vatican in Rome. I was approximately thirty-plus feet away from the side of the priest. He began to explain that on the night of Pope Francis' election he attended a celebratory mass and was given some cards to carry back to his homeland with the blessing of the Pope for two things—peace in the earth and spiritual revival and awakening in the nations. He was told as a first matter of business that, upon returning, the Lord would show him to whom he was to give these cards with the blessing of the Pope. Everyone was listening intently. He went on to say, as he walked, he had no idea to whom he was to give them, but upon approaching the microphone it became very clear to him. He gestured my way. "I am to give them to that man standing right over there against the wall." I all but completely fell out.

He gestured at me, and I responded by making my way toward him as reporters were rushing to take pictures. I literally handed my phone to a stranger on my way to meet him, and I told the lady, "Would you please take some pictures of this? Where I come from no one will ever believe this story." We chuckled, but she willingly took some great pictures. When I approached him, we spoke very casually for a couple of minutes as he inquired about what brought me to the nation's capital. I told him I was a minister and I had come to the capital to meet with global leaders contending for awakening and revival in the nations. He apologized to the reporters as he was afraid someone might think we had previously arranged this encounter. We certainly had not planned this encounter at all. He went on to tell me there was an anointing on my life for awakening, and then spoke of the Pope's work in Argentina. Originally, he was going to give me one card, but instead he felt he was to give me three cards—one for the Father, one for the Son, and one for the Holy Spirit. The card for the Holy Spirit was in Spanish, and as he left he told me we would witness a global revival and awakening. I have treasured the cards, though I am not sure I understand all that happened and why, except I believe it was confirmation of a mighty revival and awakening afoot in the nations.

Was this just another encounter? What was the Lord saying? I had more questions than answers, but it is remarkable how the Lord continues to minister to multitudes of people through amazing encounters, dreams, and visions. He is not done with the nations, and the covenant promises of God will be fulfilled. It was, nevertheless, a powerful and significant moment through which the Lord gave another piece of the puzzle on the trail to awakening. How would you have received this? How might the Lord be ministering His revelation to you in these days ahead?

Revelation received is a perceived strategy! What do I mean by that? Revelation of the Lord is a call to decisive action! Inspiration often brings with it an accompanying appreciation. I knew this encounter was a call to action! The Lord desires that we be fully functional in the operation of our faith and in the operation of our gifts. Many inspired people rejoice in the knowing but falter in the going. The Lord has called us to a life radically transformed by the power of the Holy Spirit, compelling us to live out the dynamic flow of His manifest glory upon the earth.

There must be a dismantling of inspiration that leads to idolatry and a renewed mantling of revelation that produces transformation. Transformation is radical change (see Rom. 12:1-2). I believe that there is a revelation of God being released these days that is rooted in His wisdom, manifested in His Word, and releasing His power to redeem lives, restore communities, and revive nations.

Transformational revival and true awakening always begin in the heart of a person affected by the Presence of the Lord. This means a person surrenders his heart with a radical abandonment that allows the entire life to be under the control of the Lord through the Holy Spirit. There is an abiding, an indwelling of the Holy Spirit whereby the believer is truly the host of God's Presence on the earth.

> **One thing** *have I desired of the Lord, that will I seek after; that I may dwell in the house of the Lord all the days of my life, to behold the beauty of the Lord, and to enquire in his temple* (Psalm 27:4 KJV).

Have we become satisfied to encounter His glory when He has clearly called us to embody His glory? We are on a journey not to debate the theology of the Holy Spirit in you but to release the Holy Spirit through you.

Encounters like I have described are invitations to respond to His impulses of glory. Let me share a simple outline that I will often reflect upon and consider in my daily life. I often ask myself, "Am I content to just encounter His glory, or do I desire to embody His glory?"

Encounter His glory! In John 18:1-11, we discover an amazing encounter with the Lord when Jesus asked Judas and his company bearing torches and weapons, "Whom do you seek?" They answered Him, "Jesus the

Nazarene." He said to them, "I am He." And Judas, who was betraying Him, was standing with them. When He said to them, "I am He," they drew back and fell to the ground. They fell to the ground because they encountered His glory in a bold and dramatic way, and yet we know the tragedy their choices would bring upon them afterward.

Because Judas' intention was to betray Jesus, he would never embody His glory. Nonetheless, one cannot meet Jesus without encountering His glory because Jesus Himself is one with the Father. He is "the fullness of grace and truth."

We must *embrace* His glory! In John 1:14 we read, "And the Word became flesh, and dwelt among us, and we saw His glory, glory as of the only begotten from the Father, full of grace and truth." We find here a deep and sincere recognition and an embracing of who Jesus is. Still, we need more than an acknowledgement or recognition of who He is as the Word has called us to embody His glory. We must *embody* His glory! Colossians 1:27 says, "To whom God willed to make known what is the riches of the glory of this mystery among the Gentiles, which is Christ in you, the hope of glory.". To embody the glory of God is to be made complete in Christ Jesus. There is a powerful anointing today that equips ordinary men and women to be used mightily by God. History is marked by ordinary men and women who courageously undertook mighty exploits by faith in Jesus Christ. The present and the future will be no different.

The glory of the Lord has risen upon the earth and once again the earth is about to be awakened to His manifest glory. Consider the fruit of the manifest glory of God upon the earth from Isaiah 60:1-3.

> *Arise, shine, for your light has come, and the glory of the Lord rises upon you. See, darkness covers the earth and thick darkness is over the peoples, but the Lord rises upon you and his glory appears over you. Nations will come to your light* (NIV).

1. The glory of the Lord rests upon you!
2. The glory of the Lord subdues the darkness around you!
3. The glory of the Lord will draw the lost!
4. The glory of the Lord releases provision! (See Isaiah 60:5-13.)
5. The glory of the Lord removes violence from the land! (See Isaiah 60:18.)
6. The glory of the Lord accelerates the purposes of God upon the earth! (See Isaiah 60:21-22.)

When we host the Presence of the Lord and declare the Word of the Lord, the options always change for the one who hears! When we declare His Word by the power of the Holy Spirit, the atmosphere shifts and options increase! The realm of what you see around you is the shadow of the unseen realm within you!

In Luke 7 we discover remarkable encounters with the Lord and a powerful expression of the embodiment of His Presence and glory. Let's focus on three major scenes in Luke 7.

Scene 1: We discover the faith of the centurion. The centurion turns to Jesus because he believes Jesus is sent by God. Jesus publicly shows honor to the great faith of the centurion (a Gentile) and heals his servant even from a distance. Ironically, this encounter that shows the centurion's faith in Jesus also shows God's faithfulness to us. Great faith!

Scene 2: Jesus enters Nain (a beautiful place) and sees a widow whose son has died. He is moved with compassion: "When He saw her, His heart went out to her." Then Jesus commands the boy to get up— He raises the widow's son from the dead. Those who accompany Jesus and the crowds in that city "are filled with awe and praise." Jesus brings life and restores hope to multitudes. Great hope!

Scene 3: Jesus is at the house of a synagogue official when a woman enters and begins to anoint Jesus with oil. She worships at His feet. The religious types are embarrassed because of the intimate act of worship with Jesus. But actually, that is what Jesus is looking for, rather than a religious performance. A sinful woman comes to Him in an act of worship and Jesus restores her. Like the sinful woman, our hope lies in the compassion of Christ who restores us because we are close to Him. Great love!

Chapter 7

A Pioneering Generation

Like an eagle that stirs up its nest, that hovers over its young, He spread His wings and caught them, He carried them on His pinions (Deuteronomy 32:11).

"See yourself."
Abba

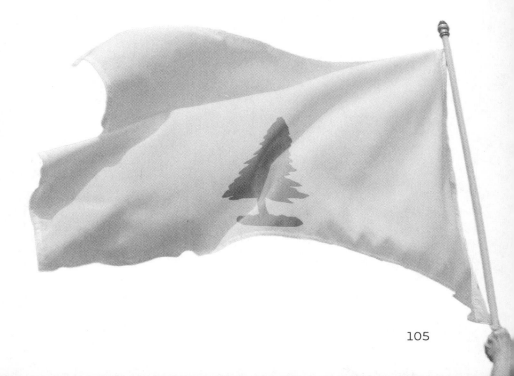

A beautiful thing happened in the wilderness of early Kentucky as the great western advance was just getting underway. We understand that fewer than 200 settlers remained in Kentucky by the spring of 1776, and most of them were in the fortified settlements of Boonesborough, Harrodsburg, and Logan's Station. On July 14, 1776, a raiding party captured three teenage girls as they were canoeing down the Kentucky River outside the safe walls of Boonesborough. Two of the girls, Elizabeth and Francis, were the daughters of Colonel Richard Callaway. The other girl was Jemima Boone, the daughter of the famed American frontiersman Daniel Boone. The girls were being carried away into captivity and were certainly afraid. However, Jemima knew her father would come searching until he found them. As the girls were being carried away. Jemima had the strong mind about her to literally rip off pieces of her dress and leave them strewn along the path to mark the trail for her father and his accompanying party to find them more easily. The plan worked beautifully. The girls were rescued without harm.

Pioneering Vision
Revisits the Foundations

The girls were desperate, but they knew their fathers would be coming for them. Likewise, I believe although we are living in desperate times, we too can be confident the Father is coming in the wild pursuit of this generation. A distinguishing mark of each pioneering generation is pioneering vision for the days that lie ahead. It is simply how history moves forward. Vision always leads forward into the storyline of history. Each generation struggles with conflicted visions of tomorrow and the understanding of history. Markers, like torn pieces of a primitive dress, are marking the trail to lead the Father straight toward this generation.

Vision renews the original mission and calling. We are in a moment of significant cultural shifts. Awakening demands revisiting the foundations of faith and important events that took place along the path. We must dream of a bolder and more brilliant expression of the Church in the future. The great commission embraces the power of the Holy Spirit to advance the cause of Christ once again to the nations.

Get ready for a mighty outpouring of the Holy Spirit in Pentecostal power that produces breakthrough for generations and marks the trail today for tomorrow's followers.

Pioneering Vision Restores the Fundamentals

Is awakening underway in measures that seem small and in hearts increasingly desperate? Will we see a bold return to a simple faith producing a profound movement of God in the nations? Is a remnant Church arising with surrendered lives and submitted hearts abandoning themselves afresh at the feet of the Savior? The answer to these questions will determine the future of vital Christianity in America.

There are revivals today developing into sustainable moves of God that can lead us into awakening in regions and nations. Listen closely and you will hear the sound of dancing like muffled raindrops on a tin roof. The heralds have their songs muted by the chaotic noise of a confused generation, but make no mistake, they are still singing. The Spirit of awakening is in the land.

There are those who believe it is time for a dark and melancholy dirge to be sung over the nation. Have we moved so far from the benchmarks of our spiritual and moral underpinnings that we can no longer anticipate a glorious move of God? Has the United States forfeited her glorious opportunity to lead in a global awakening, or is the melancholy sound of the despairing about to become the jubilant song of the redeemed? Are we beginning to witness the fire of God kindle a sacred enthusiasm in the hearts and lives of ordinary men and women?

There has been prevailing intercession and profound prophetic utterance released in a myriad of settings as the current generation becomes increasingly desperate for revival. One consistent cry has been for the ancient wells of revival and awakening in the land to be opened once again and the nation to encounter the manifest glory of God in the power of a pervasive move of God. The sounds of the early stages of awakening can be heard in the land.

There must be a return to the fundamentals of *humility*, *honor*, and *holiness*. How desperately we need a fresh move of God that restores authentic humility in the hearts of leaders willing to honor and prefer others better than themselves. This is a bold return to the fundamentals. We must contend for the synergistic relationship in the Spirit between generations and serve one another in humility. We have increasingly become a culture without honor, but this must be addressed by the Church—not with placards and marches but with honesty, confession, and sincerity. We need each other far more than the time we live as though we do.

We are desperate to renew the revelation of the holiness of God. Holiness should not be legalistic and divisive but quite the opposite. Holiness means freedom and unifying. Holiness is the revelation of the Father's heart for the weary and broken. I remember as a small boy kneeling beside my Papaw's green vinyl couch as he placed his strong hands on my head and prayed that I would all the days of my life "follow peace with all men, and holiness, without which no man shall see the Lord" (Heb. 12:14 KJV). He was praying for the Father's heart to be manifest in my life. He was praying for the foundations of my life to be reflective of God's will and purpose. He was praying for the fire of His holiness to burn brightly in me and shape my life for God's providential purpose. Now as I reflect back on him, I think how priceless it would be to have his hands placed on my head just one more time. Blessing the generations that come after us is powerful and it is a necessity to do so. Please, let's not label the destiny of the next generation by the dysfunction of our own. Let's model humility. Let's give honor. Let's run after the bold fire of the holiness of God that cleanses the heart and empowers life for service.

Pioneering Vision Releases Faith for the Future

Lightning and power are returning to the Church. During the Welsh revival it was often said that the Holy Ghost speaks through men, but often it is in the quiet. He reveals Himself to the true plight of the human heart. When we allow the Holy Ghost to visit us in the private chamber of our prayer, He will often manifest His power in public. As we kneel before the Lord in the quietness of our prayer closet, we experience the quickening of the Holy Spirit.

Listen to this personal account of the Spirit's work during the Welsh revival:

> In the light of His purity, it was not so much sin we saw as self. We saw pride and self-motives underlying everything we had ever done. Lust and self-pity were discovered in places where we had never suspected them. And we had to confess we knew nothing of the Holy Ghost as an indwelling Person. That our bodies were meant to be the temples of the Holy Ghost we knew, but when He pressed the question, "Who is living in your body?" we could not say that He was. We would have done so once, but now we have seen Him.[1]

The storyline of history is often scribed through the lives of ordinary men and women. Pioneering vision releases great faith to overcome every obstacle, stand in every trial, and boldly mark the path into a brilliant future. History has been marked by the expressions of faith and simple exploits of courage in the lives of many men and women. Could it be that once again in the future history will be written from the lives of the ordinary ones today? God's providence moves in the lives of the ordinary ones and shapes a better future for all who would follow, and here we may find principles that will reveal hope for today and a brighter tomorrow—our tomorrow.

A Pioneering Generation

"Like an eagle that stirs up its nest, that hovers over its young, He spread His wings and caught them, He carried them on His pinions" (Deut. 32:11). The fierce revelation of the *love of God* and of *His mercy* to shape history through the lives of common people is what the world loathes and yet longs to hear again.

The days in which we live demand the emergence of a new pioneering generation. Make no mistake about it, the young people appearing today in amazing creative style and heart will be a generation that marks history for the glory of God. A pioneering generation is always a generation that confronts the wilderness of their time and champions a bolder and brighter way forward.

Dreams are often pioneering visions that bring clarity of assignments and provide revelation for prayer and intercession. I had a dream on March 1, 2012, and it continues to bring hope and insight into how we are learning to steward our assignments in ministry and bring hope to the awakening of a nation. Here is the dream.

A Governmental Dream: The Third Floor: The White House, Washington, DC

During the early morning hours today, March 1, 2012, I had a dream that I feel is directly connected with a series of dreams I have had previously of America's next great awakening.

I dreamed that I was returning to the White House for a strategic gathering. In the dream it was unclear who would be in attendance, but I traveled alone to the nation's capital. Upon arriving in Washington, DC, I spent the night prior to the appointed time for arrival in a local hotel. I do not know the name of the hotel, but it appeared to be an older and very historic hotel very near the White House. It was very swank and sophisticated, and I had a suite that included a balcony overlooking the grounds of the White House and the surrounding area. Others were staying in the same hotel though I did not know that when I arrived. As a matter of fact, after arriving I went down to the restaurant to eat dinner and I saw a couple of friends sitting at a table near the corner of the room. They invited me to sit with them. While sitting at their table, we were joined by two more who had entered the restaurant. They joined us at the table, but I don't recall anything about the conversation. I just knew we were all at the table sharing a meal. I do not know if we were given instructions to go to that specific place or not, but it seemed important and strategic.

Upon arriving at the White House, I was greeted at the gate and led through security into the mansion itself. I was immediately taken to the third floor of the White House. The escort was a well-dressed gentleman in a business suit. While taking the staircase up to the third floor, he cautioned me to always use the stairs upon entering, that I was not to trust the elevators. He also said he would tell the others as well. I was escorted up the steps that brought me out into a large central hallway with rooms off to each side. The rooms seemed to vary in size and intent—some bedrooms, offices, sitting rooms, and a room with a large round conference table. I was escorted to a room where I was told I would be sleeping. I was to place all personal belongings in this room and could be assured they were perfectly safe. The room would also be a place where I would study, pray, or spend any necessary private time. It was elegant but not overly gaudy or sophisticated.

The escort pointed out to me the brief historical significance of each of the rooms as we passed by them. When I arrived at the room that I would be staying in, I was given a little bit of the history of the room and was told the bed was that of President John Adams. The escort asked me if I knew anything about the life and presidency of John Adams. I told him very little. I said, "He was the second president of the United States; his vice president was rival Thomas Jefferson (and I knew Jefferson beat him in his reelection bid); his was the first father and son duo to serve the presidency (John Q. Adams, son)." Further, I admitted that I was not that informed as to the life and the presidency of John Adams.

I was then shown portions of the rest of the third floor. There were rooms near the end of the hallway that had been developed into offices where we would have access to communication tools and all necessary equipment. There were also additional bedrooms, bathrooms, and some more casual rooms for sitting. In addition, there was a room that had a large round conference table where meetings would be held.

There were several others also gathering on the third floor. Some of them I knew. Some I did not. Upon exiting the room, I walked into the hallway, and I saw a large window with a domed top to it and two men standing in front of the window looking out. I recognized one of the men standing to the right of the other man. I stood and looked at them for a moment. They had joined hands and had raised their two hands that were being held straight up in the air. Their other two arms were raised up and I knew they were praying and making prophetic decrees out the window over the capital city and the nation.

As I walked up behind them all the other people who were on the floor came and we stood together just behind them, and we all entered a prolonged period of intercession and prophetic decree. Finally, the two of them turned and faced us standing in the hallway. The minister said, "Gentlemen, it is time to move! We must now establish the Ekklesia and begin the process of restoring the republic." Immediately, as he said that the gentleman who had escorted me to the third floor stepped into the picture from my left, and he said to the entire group, "With that command I am now released to make a presentation. The time for this assignment is now." So, he turned toward these leaders and handed them a seal of the president of the United States. The ministers lifted the seal high, holding it between them. The room was immediately engulfed in silence, and it seemed to be a very serious moment.

The prophet began to interpret a message given in tongues. His hands were raised up and he was making prophetic declarations concerning winds of change and rebuilding of the republic. We were coming into agreement as we stood silently before them. Major downloads were coming to the leaders of the prophetic and apostolic ministries. We could see smoke in the distance rising from some of the buildings and repairs being made in the presence of guards to the fence surrounding the White House grounds. The gates had been overrun by mobs of people and the fences crossed, violating the grounds of the official residence. The Lord spoke to me that there will be a great increase in both the *scope and the specificity of forthcoming revelation* in this apostolic-prophetic reformation.

Numerous meetings were held during the dream. Roundtable meetings wherein strategy was developed were held regularly. Cooperation among the apostolic and prophetic meetings increased along with all the necessary expressions of the fivefold ministries. We began to traverse in and out of the White House grounds on specific assignments. Interestingly, we were instructed without exception that we were to use the staircase rather than the elevator to access the third floor.

As the dream concluded I was backing away, and I could see prayer and intercession, intimate worship, and a nation-shifting prophetic decree rising from the White House. The dream ended.

The influence of media and an endless barrage of images, which we are confronted with every day, can produce great fear and anxiety, anger, division, and violence. However, we must allow the Lord to reveal truth to rise above the despair and believe God for His bold awakening in our day. This awakening in the lives of ordinary men and women will once again pioneer a vision of hope and faith for generations to come.

Note

1. Dr. Kingsley Priddy, qtd. in Normal Grubb, *Rees Howells: Intercessor* (Fort Washington, PA: Christian Literature Crusade, 1996), 250-251.

Chapter 8

Are You Ready to Take Your Place?

Do not despise these small beginnings, for the Lord rejoices to see the work begin (Zechariah 4:10 NLT).

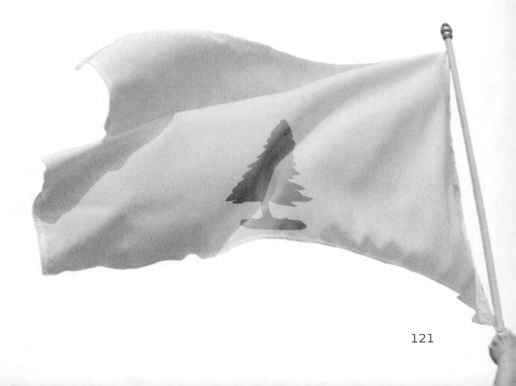

The storyline of history is often scribed through the lives of ordinary men and women. History has been marked by the bold expressions of faith and simple exploits of courage in the lives of many men and women. It is a most interesting and rewarding endeavor to look back to history and discover how the hand of God's providence moved in the lives of the ordinary ones and shaped a better future for all who would follow. We often discover principles that will reveal hope for today and a brighter tomorrow—our tomorrow. You will find such people everywhere you look. Watch for them. Are you ready to take your place in the storyline of history?

I met such an amazing person in a most remarkable place. Jennifer and I were invited to go to the White House in Washington, DC to join in the prayer efforts the nation organized through the National Day of Prayer. We were very excited by this opportunity. When we arrived, I am sure our behavior was like most who visit this beautiful house for the first time. We were welcomed inside where we had a wonderful breakfast of pastries and interesting delicacies. They invited us to make ourselves at home that morning, so Jennifer and I enjoyed going room to room and taking in all the sights and sharing in wonderful conversation. Suddenly, I told Jennifer I wanted to walk downstairs and explore the lower level a little. She did not believe that was a good idea and decided she would stay upstairs. I walked slowly down the steps, and at the landing at the lower level made a left turn down a long hall and almost immediately ran into the library inside the White House. I did not need to go any further. I stepped inside the library and just began to look at books on the shelves and the beautiful furniture, and I gazed out the window and wondered how I really got here. We knew we were on assignment, and the leading of the Holy Spirit would always take us on rich adventures. I felt the spirit of prayer come on me, so I just started walking around the room praying quietly and enjoying the surroundings.

Suddenly, I looked up and there were two men standing shoulder to shoulder in the middle of the doorway. I was a little startled. One of the men was a young officer sharply dressed in formal military attire. The other was an elderly gentleman dressed in a perfectly fitting tuxedo. When I saw them my first response was, "Oh, should I not be in here?" All I could think about was Jennifer who had warned me that if I got into trouble, she wouldn't know me. I knew she didn't mean that, but I was seriously questioning my decision at that point. The young officer never spoke, but the elderly man, a

White House butler, answered quickly and told me, "No sir, it is fine. I knew someone was in here praying!"

Now, my meter for adventure was escalating dramatically and I felt excited as if he had more to say. He continued telling me he was a part of an intercessory prayer group of people who work every day in this home serving the presidents of the United States. Furthermore, he stated there had been an unbroken chain of intercessors working and praying in this home for over 150 years. I simply marveled at all he had to tell me about this.

I invited him into the room to pray with me. I wanted to stand with him in the storyline of those who serve the nation and our presidents and families on the frontlines in this beautiful place. At first, he was very hesitant and told me he would not enter the room if I was in it, but with some persuasion he stepped in, and we prayed and rejoiced over the rich history of our nation and even this specific room. What were the chances of our meeting? He told me, I have no reason to know if this is true or not, that this room, the library, was President Reagan's favorite room in the house and that the red color on the walls in the bookcases is the color President Reagan picked out.

Why am I including that story? I want you to know the sound of awakening is being heard across the land through people praying, loving, and winning the day by faithfully serving in their place of ministry. We focus so much on the platform ministry, but I am confident the coming move of God will be a grassroots movement of God igniting the hearts of ordinary men and women. These will find their voice and become a wonderful contribution to the expanding hope that lies at the heart of the nation. Allow God to use you freely in the very place you serve. By the way, the elderly butler wept with me in the library as he shared his deep concern for the days that lay ahead for the nation. Friend, hope is not lost and, in fact, nations are being divinely poised for another great awakening. This time it will be organic, grassroots, and will rest on the foundation of humility, honor, and holiness or the heart of the Father for lost and broken humanity.

These champions and heralds are among us, and once again we will find ordinary men and women stepping quietly out of places of seclusion and into a place of significance in history. When history loses its urgency, people have the greatest tendency to live at the expense of the future.

History is often shaped by one person touching the life of another, setting off a series of unexpected events. History is told one story, one person, one decision, or one action at a time. The great attraction of Christianity throughout history is a transformed life full of love, devotion, and courage. A life saved by Christ and energized by His love is a contagious testimony of a transformed life.

Dynamic moments of history happen when God moves among men who may not perceive their broader significance. People are writing history through acts of courage and selfless deeds of service. Supernatural miracles may be ignited by a simple decision.

I love the story of Edward Kimball, an ordinary man whom God would use to unlock a series of events that would impact hundreds of millions of people around the world. He led a young teenage boy, who was a part of his Sunday school class, to the Lord while visiting him in a shoe shop where the young boy was working. That boy was D.L. Moody who would go on to minister to more than 100 million people. He would also begin the Moody Bible Church and the Moody Institute in Chicago.

D.L. Moody would be very influential in leading a young man, Dr. Wilbur Chapman, to the Lord. Dr. Chapman was in large part responsible for influencing the fiery evangelist and professional baseball player Billy Sunday to give his life to the Lord. Billy Sunday was one of the most powerful evangelists of his day. He would lead Mordecai Ham, a powerful preacher from Kentucky, to the Lord! Mordecai Ham was preaching the night that young Billy Graham gave his heart to the Lord. Billy Graham preached the Gospel of Jesus Christ to more people than any other man in history. Kimbal's gift to the Kingdom of God began on a small platform of a Sunday school class, but resulted in an evangelistic thrust and millions coming to know the Lord.

It's amazing how large the platform of a consecrated and willing heart! One story, one life, one decision influenced by the love of God and the Holy Spirit can change millions of lives all over the world.

I am writing this dream at 8:52 AM on February 6, 2018. I have penned it in my journal and now I record it here.

The Dream

As I lay in my bed last evening, I was awakened at 1:38 AM processing this dream. I dreamed there were people in my living room. I dreamed that it was full of people, and I felt it was a gathering of past generations. I got up in the dream and walked into the living room to see who was there. When I walked in, I thought it was my living room. I walked into a very large coliseum type structure that was massive and completely packed with people. The gathering was so massive, it was as though there were incredible overflows that reached all the way to the horizon. The expansive gathering was amazing, and the people were all sitting quietly and watching intently.

The lighting was not good, and the faces of the multitudes were obscured by the dimly lit space. Upon entering the coliseum, I noticed a very large stage with a single chair placed in the middle of the space. It looked like my Welsh chair, so I naturally walked toward the chair. I suddenly felt this was a follow-up dream to the "Appeal to Heaven" dream. As I looked over the expansive gathering of people, I could tell immediately I was looking at generations! They were young and old. The gathering was very quiet. Suddenly, I felt a strong impression, "It is not what you think it is!"

I remember thinking in the dream that this was once again a dream of the generations who had gone before us, but it was not. Then I saw a stirring among the people out at the distant horizon of the gathering, and I heard a loud proclamation:

"There is *One* to whom all generations will bow!"

I saw the Lord walking from the rear of the gathering. He was walking on what appeared to be water suspended above the ground and completely engulfed by the light of His glory! As He walked, the crowds separated before Him, and as He passed, the people became as a wave bowing low before His passing. I remember thinking in the dream the bows of the people made it look as though they were "folding in half" and all ended up on the floor. He walked slowly and all bowed before Him.

As the Lord made His way among the people, I could see above Him a light brilliantly shining and increasing in size as He approached. It was as though the light above Him was tremulous and loving like the waves of the sea. I could then see He was accompanied by a massive and fierce Angel Army hovering over His head and stirring the hearts of the people as He passed by them. I could hear a faint and distant sound echoing, "Holy, Holy, Holy!" I then heard for a second time:

"THERE IS *ONE* TO WHOM ALL GENERATIONS WILL BOW!"

As the Lord, accompanied by this Angel Army, approached the center front of the gathering the brilliant radiance of His glory lit up the faces of those gathered and I was told:

> These are not just the generations who went before you, but these are the generations who will come after you! These are future generations. These are the young and the not yet born.
>
> These are those who will come out of grave darkness and into the glorious light of the Lord for the purpose of supernatural exploits in the Kingdom.
>
> These are generations in waiting and training who will be summoned to synergy, releasing

global moves of God producing the greatest harvest the world has ever seen.

These are generations who will embrace the accompanying force of heaven's armies and will partner with the Holy Spirit for the manifest glory of the Lord in the earth.

They will come before Him and encounter Him in holy awe bowing low in worship, and they will arise as no generation before them.

They will arise in the manifest light of His glory, and the Lord said, "Even now, you will begin to see it with your own eyes!"

The Lord ministered to me that my own ministry was to change and, in fact, I was to begin to watch ministries shift emphasis in many ways to lead a generation into a bold encounter with Him! Watch for the ministry to be more reflective of:

1. **His holiness**: the brilliance of His glory, the beauty of His nature, the depths of His transforming love, and the unfathomable power of the Holy Spirit. Creative miracles will begin, and watch for the rebirth of the *missions movement* to begin! A bold and courageous generation is emerging that will do exploits the likes of

which past generations could have never imagined!

2. **His heart**: the expanse of His love, the depths of His grace, and the power of His manifest justice in the earth. Global shifts and political structures are being tested and they will bow to the unyielding witness of a generation of millennials impacting a millennium!

3. **His hand**: in the dream the Lord would simply gesture with His hand and generations would bow before Him. Watch for harvests to be won where there is no stage or even a preacher. Watch for His hand to move upon nations, regions, tribes, and peoples around the world who will begin to be transformed by a simple response to one manifestation of the great hand of the Lord. Watch for true synergy and powerful creative miracles.

I heard the Lord say we have passed the test and that we are about to witness what He has promised generations! The times in which we are living may on one hand become darker, more violent, and even more extreme; *however*, the Lord has raised up this generation for precisely this moment. The greatest Kingdom advancement will come in a season marked by unrest, instability, violence, and extremism. He is summoning a generation to *arise and ascend* and to take their place.

Are you ready to take your place in the storyline of history? Are you ready to become a part of the remnant Church and believe God once again for a bold display of signs, wonders, and miracles? Will you be a part of winning a mighty harvest for God?

Chapter 9

An Awakening Mosaic

Behold, how good and how pleasant it is for brothers to dwell together in unity! It is like precious oil upon the head, coming down upon the beard, even Aaron's beard, coming down upon the edge of his robes (Psalm 133:1-2).

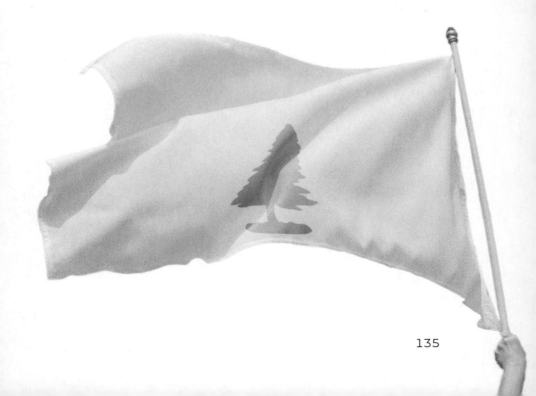

135

The subtle embrace of night casts her shadow across the brow of the young maiden of liberty. Night's luring embrace seems to seduce the nation further into an abyss of compromise slouching toward chaos. The brilliant hope of the nations and the grand experiment of self-governance "by the people and for the people" reels from her confusion and compromise. America is staggering from compromised values, confusing and unsustainable standards, and a glamorized chaos. Where is the leadership compelled by a vision for America's future that is truly worthy of her good past? Where are the champions of mercy and the heralds of brotherly love? Where are those who will lay down their lives to bring us together and stand for a cause greater than themselves? These champions and heralds are among us, and once again we will find ordinary men and women stepping quietly out of places of seclusion and into historical significance. When history loses its urgency, people have the greatest tendency to live at the expense of the future.

History is often shaped by one person touching the life of another, setting off a series of events that no one could have perceived. The brilliance of history is powerfully told one story, one person, one decision, or one action at a time. The great attraction of Christianity is the lure of a transformed life—radiant in love, brilliant in personality, devoted in service, and contagious in enthusiasm. Simply put, a life burning for God. A life miraculously saved by the gift of the Lord Jesus Christ. A life boldly spent as the burning energy of this supreme love.

The magnificent history of God moving mightily among men introduces us to ordinary men and women living in dynamic moments of history—often without perceiving the broader significance of their times. Many today are writing history through bold acts of courage and selfless deeds of service. Sometimes the most compelling, and might we say supernatural, things that occur often begin with a simple decision that may look innocent enough or even mundane.

The awakening at hand will not be carried on the backs of great gatherings and services but will be carried in the hearts and lives of ordinary men and women stewarding the Presence of God and not just performing good services. Watch for a grassroots awakening that will once again give birth to a new discipleship movement. Recently, I wrote in my journal a word I felt to be of the Lord: "There is an unstoppable hunger for the unquenchable fire of God!" This hunger is to be discipled and trained, equipped, and released to fulfill the mandate of Christ in the nations. Ordinary men and women are coming together for a cause greater than any one of them can accomplish individually.

Listen for the sound of awakening to be released through the lives of everyday and ordinary men and women in the streets of our cities, the fields of our farmlands, and churches scattered all over the land. Open fields will become sanctuaries, and homes will become houses of prayer. Those who have been ignored or overlooked will ascend to a place of dramatic effectiveness in the Kingdom of God. This awakening will have many similar expressions of previous moves of God, but it will also carry a uniqueness in the earth that is reflective of this generation.

How do we prepare? How do we sustain an awakening? How do we train and equip a generation? Is it time for America's awakening? If so, we must not delay another moment in preparing ourselves and a generation of leaders to champion the cause of Christ in this mighty awakening. One encounter that was a powerful witness to us of the nearness of this awakening happened in an unlikely place at a totally unsuspecting time.

I had been invited to speak at a conference in Virginia Beach. The conference was being sponsored by people with whom Jennifer and I were not familiar, but it was a most pleasant experience and a powerful conference. One morning the agenda included a prayer trip to Cape Henry not far from the conference location. We were very excited to go to Cape Henry as we had never visited the site before. It was a very cool morning that felt much colder because of rain and heavy wind, but we were not about to cancel the trip.

Upon arriving at Cape Henry, the weather just became worse with the increase of winds and rain. When we arrived at the parking lot near the Cape Henry Memorial, my wife, along with a friend traveling with us, was reluctant to get out of the vehicle. This was the site of the first landfall of colonists bound for the Jamestown settlement in 1607. It is a remarkable place that is vital in understanding the storyline of American history. I was not about to let the wind and rain keep me from walking out on the pier that I might celebrate this wonderful site. The date of our visit was the anniversary date of the actual landing in 1607.

While standing on the wooden pier, I was taking pictures with my camera and reflecting upon the generations who had gone before us. Their sense of vision, purpose, and great passion for freedom and the cause of Christ in the earth is always incredible to me. As I was taking pictures, suddenly I was aware of movement behind me, and then I heard a lady say, "Excuse me, sir, may I speak with you a moment?" I turned and saw three ladies standing there with banners and flags praying upon the land. The lady continued by telling me a story of how God had sent them on a prayer assignment to Virginia Beach. She said they had arrived that morning and had gone for the taping of a show at

Christian Broadcasting Network. While there, they had received a prophetic word from an internationally recognized Christian leader who had mentioned to them that they were to come to Cape Henry and there they would meet a man. He further stated they were to give the man a message. They told me because I was the only man present, they were certain the word must be for me. We laughed together and I welcomed the word the ladies had to share. It was a simple and yet timely word. I was stunned by it. Let me be clear, I had never seen these ladies before, and I knew nothing about them, nor did they have any idea who I was or why I was there.

The word they shared with me was this: "*The appeal has been heard, and it is time for America's awakening to begin!*" That was it. I asked them if they had any knowledge of the "Appeal to Heaven" dream and had they become aware of it and the movement birthed through the dream. They said they had read Dutch Sheets' book entitled *An Appeal to Heaven*, but they had no idea I was the one who had the dream. We often read of past revivals and awakenings, but what will it be like in our generation? It is time to find out.

A few years ago, Jennifer and I were ministered to by a nationally recognized minister who released a powerful vision of the Lord over our lives. He said that he could see us accelerating in the Spirit at an amazing rate and that the Lord was releasing upon our lives an anointing for strategy and awakening in the nations. He said that he could see the Lord giving us a blueprint to build a model for sustaining revival and carrying awakening to the nations. The model would not be theologically or philosophically focused but would be practically taught and implemented in the lives of ordinary men and women. This minister had no knowledge of the angel encounter in Argentina, and this was precisely the assignment I felt was being released upon our lives while in Argentina years earlier. Immediately, I felt the Lord confirm this word in me with an image of a beautiful mosaic of broken glass fitly formed by the hands of a master artist.

What I saw was *an Awakening Mosaic,* a masterful design of the Lord to bring together leaders from all the offices of ministry and expressions of the Kingdom. The mosaic is made up of leaders who are like the broken pieces of glass—some even have sharp edges, but are perfectly formed together by the hands of the Master Artist. We received this word and this assignment and have turned ourselves toward it since that time. An Awakening Mosaic is a unique strategy for rebirthing a mission of evangelism and discipleship in the nations.

At the heart of the Awakening Mosaic is the firm conviction that America's, and indeed the world's, greatest awakening lies before us and not behind us. We are living in an unprecedented time that provides unparalleled opportunities. We share dramatic accounts of ordinary people being used by the Lord. One of the fantastic discoveries in history for me is the remarkable events that can unfold through a series of very small and seemingly insignificant events.

Through the Awakening Mosaic strategy, we seek to mobilize a generation of ordinary men and women, and together we will unlock that which has been restricting revival in America and beyond! This mosaic strategy will allow for a grassroots movement in the nation to arise like a gusher. The coming revival will change the course of the land, and it must begin with leaders willing to labor together as never before.

In the "Appeal to Heaven" dream one of the most powerful moments was when I was asked the question, "Are you ready to take your place in the storyline of history?" I knew as I penned the dream in my journal that the question was not for me only, but for all who will hear the quickening word of the Lord. So the question is yours as much as it is mine. Are you ready? Are you willing to take your place? Will you connect, cooperate, and cross-pollinate with leaders from around the nation for a united cause?

An Awakening Mosaic

Creating Synergy

> syn·er·gy \ ˈsi-nər-jē: a mutually advanta-
> geous conjunction or compatibility of dis-
> tinct participants

Awakening Mosaic Vision: The vision of the Awakening Mosaic is to connect leaders relationally for the cause of awakening our communities and our nation. We can easily accept the status quo of spiritual life in the nation, and make excuses concerning our differences that distance us. We can readily defend the culture of dysfunction that these differences often breed, or we can connect for better and stronger communities. Indeed, a nation shaped for her brightest future by leaders who humbly acknowledge the mission of America's greatest awakening can never be accomplished alone.

Awakening Mosaic Cause: The Awakening Mosaic is for the cause of Christ and His commission. It is for an awakening that produces the fruit of an unprecedented harvest in the nations of the earth. Generational awakening must be carried on the backs of courageous leaders willing to inspire people to believe in what God can do in us, not just what the government can do for us. This generational awakening begins, simply put, at our willingness to connect for a "cause" so great it demands the courage of our connectivity and the strength of our synergy.

Awakening Mosaic Benchmarks: What is a benchmark? "A fixed point of reference from which all other essential components can be measured" (*Merriam-Webster*). The weight of the covering is measured by the strength of the foundation. The foundational benchmarks for an Awakening Mosaic are simple—*humility, honor, and holiness* (heart of the Father).

These benchmarks determine the posture of relational synergy:

1. We humble ourselves first before the Father, asking Him to give us an honest assessment of our motives and intentions for His assignment in the nation, and we humble ourselves before one another. Our connectivity is facilitated through the spirit of our humility.

   - We humble ourselves in a spirit of repentance and confession.
   - We humble ourselves desiring to see His heart for the hopelessness many people carry in their lives.
   - We humble ourselves as we desire His increase in our appetite for His

Presence, His power, and His favor for the nations.

2. We honor the Lord, and we honor one another.

- The seat of honor in all our mosaic gatherings belongs to the Lord, and we will never be apologetic for His Word and His work among us.

- Honor creates a culture of intentional connectivity and synergy.

- Honor cultivates synergy in diversity.

3. We serve from the posture of the Father's heart.

- What is the perspective of the Father's heart for the plight of humanity and the predicament of the Church? Considering your answer, what posture should we take as a response?

- What does the Father feel over the anguish of suffering, the pain of rebellion, or the hopelessness of addiction and poverty? If we were intentional about our alignment with His heart and our willingness to act

courageously together, could we see
hope restored in this generation?

As we share in the anguish of the broken heart
of God for wounded humanity, we will rejoice with
Him as He draws the masses into a place of awakening
and revival.

God moves through people motivated by a spirit
of servanthood. This servanthood was most powerfully manifested through the life and ministry priorities
of Jesus:

> *You will lead by a completely different model.
> The greatest one among you will live as the
> one who is called to serve others, because the
> greatest honor and authority is reserved for
> the one with the heart of a servant. For even
> the Son of Man did not come expecting to be
> served but to serve and give his life in exchange
> for the salvation of many* (Matthew 20:26-28
> TPT).
>
> *Mobilize! The enemy lays siege* (Micah 5:1
> TLB).

Releasing Strategy

strat·e·gy \ -jē: the skill of making or carrying out plans to achieve a goal or fulfill a
purpose

A foundational principle of Mosaic is that the awakening coming to the nation will not be carried on the energy of good worship gatherings alone. It must be carried in the hearts of committed leaders who are willing to serve others in the cause of this greatest awakening. We have seen in the last seven years at least five revivals that have each been extended to a year or more through this ministry of connecting leaders for a cause greater than themselves. The hunger that is so prevalent in the Church today is very real in pastors and leaders. We need a people who can entrust themselves to one another and to the will of God.

What if the Church today could abandon past patterns of competition and comparison for the joy of collaboration and connection? It would be incredible to see the Church once again champion the cause of Christ in winning the lost and making disciples rather than guarding territories and agendas.

When the Spirit of God begins to sweep across the land awakening the hearts and transforming the lives of many everyday people, He brings them into a fresh realization that He desires to use them mightily in this move. What does this personal awakening look like?

Chapter 10

A Remnant Rising

Arise, shine; for your light has come, and the glory of the Lord has risen upon you. For behold, darkness will cover the earth and deep darkness the peoples; but the Lord will rise upon you and His glory will appear upon you. Nations will come to your light, and kings to the brightness of your rising (Isaiah 60:1-3).

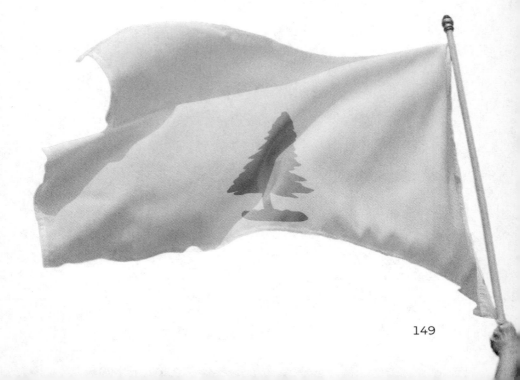

The dawn of America's greatest awakening must be hastened through travailing intercession and bold acts of courage. History is marked by Christian communities that thrived miraculously well in days of dark and tragic adversity. History is also marked by those who didn't fare so well and, in fact, utterly failed.

Many examples of persistent fruitfulness and peculiar failures could be charted along the trail of history. It is imperative we walk this trail and be reminded of the principles that lead a nation into generational synergy and authentic awakening. Maybe we could borrow from the title of one of Charles Olson's poems: "The Chain of Memory Is Resurrection." It is by remembrance we release the hope that rests with the fathers and mothers beneath the ground upon which we now walk.

I am stricken by the words of Dr. Philip Jenkins who seriously pined while writing so effectively about the history of Christianity and why the Church has never developed a "theology of extinction." Extinction? Is it possible for the faith of a people, whether a nation or a community, to be so decimated by a series of incalculable events that faith completely disappears in any form of practical and biblical relevance?

The Coptic Christians in Egypt are an example of Christian resilience through many generations and innumerable threats in dark times of political unrest and regime madness. In an April 2017 article in *Christianity Today* by Jason Casper entitled "Forgiveness: Muslims Moved as Coptic Christians Do the Unimaginable," the author pursues fundamental principles that lie at the root of the Coptic Christians—strength and power through weakness and forgiveness. The world was amazed to watch the Coptic Christians respond to horrific terrorist attacks upon their own churches and families. It was a powerful and pervasive response. They responded with forgiveness and in that, found a resurgence of hope and healing. "Since then, there has been a paradigm shift," said Ramez Atallah. "Our ancestors lived and believed this message, but we never had to."[1]

In comparison to the faithful persistence of the Coptic Church, the African Church was, in its day, one of the wonders of the Christian world. Theodor Mommsen once wrote, "In the development of Christianity, Africa plays the first part. If it arose in Syria, it was in and through Africa that it became the religion of the world."[2] Africa was home to incredible early leaders like Tertullian, Cyprian, and Augustine. "North Africa in the century after 560 was a potent center of spiritual, literary, and cultural activity: 'in no part of the West were the clergy and people so orthodox as in Africa.'"[3] Yet by 698 and within 50 years of the completion of the Arab conquest, "local Muslim rulers were apologizing to the caliphs that they could no longer supply Christian slaves, since Christians were now so scarce."[4]

Pioneers carve paths that become a trail first, and then a road, and finally a superhighway. We traveled along with ministry partners to El Camino Real from the border in El Paso, Texas into the heart of New Mexico, releasing the fire of awakening along the nation's first superhighway, the King's Highway! Extraordinary events unfolded along t a mason's tool in one hand and a sword in the other, refusing to come off the wall. We learn to honor and prefer others better than ourselves as we serve, build, and encourage others to their place of ministry and service. We return to the Lord in repentance and in complete surrender. We must train, equip, empower, and send a generation of evangelists and revivalists in all the fields of service.

The equipping and empowering of future generations will be swift and unconventional. We are witnessing a rapid increase in the unfolding of prophetic events that point us toward the reaping of a global harvest of souls. The Lord is governing the affairs of men and drawing generations into the hope of His glorious coming. Once again, God is "taking the work into His own hands." I love this quote attributed to Jonathan Edwards in the First Great Awakening: "When God, in so remarkable a manner, took the work into His own hands, there was as much done in a day or two, as at ordinary times...is done in a year."

The Future Generations

How did Christianity arise and spread so rapidly among nations and peoples? Did Christianity expand by institutions, establishments of mechanical systems? The answer is a resounding, "No!" Carlyle once powerfully wrote, "It flew like hallowed fire fanned from heart to heart until all were purified and illumined by it." It was the sacred flame of love that marked the secret success and the bold evangelizing of the world in the early Church. I propose the same is true today! A life saturated by the sacred flame of love and lived for the glory of God as a gift to others will still mark history in unforgettable ways.

There is an ascending generation of young people who will be powerful in ways generations before them failed to be. People often look at the young generations that are coming up behind them and judge them harshly and very wrongly. There is a tendency to judge the upcoming generations with the dysfunction that was prevalent in the older or previous generations. The dysfunction of the older will not become the function of the younger. The Lord has preserved a remnant who will do mighty exploits in the Kingdom of God and perform bold acts of courage, restoring the fear of the Lord and the hope of generations. What if we were at the place of the greatest awakening the nation has ever known? Where would it begin? What would it cost? How remarkable would the lives become that were transformed by the power of the Holy Spirit in another great awakening? There is an unstoppable hunger for the unquenchable fire of God in this young generation, but the expression of this fire will be seen vividly in bold deeds of service and powerful acts of courage.

When the end of a long and dreadful night gives way to the brilliance of a sunrise, the hearts of the people rejoice. We are now experiencing such a sunrise in America. The appeal has been heard and it's time for America's greatest awakening. Didn't Ruth lie at the feet of her kinsman redeemer until morning came? In this story of Boaz and Ruth, we are reminded of God's redemptive purposes.

1. The Lord *delivers* from slavery! (See Leviticus 25:48.)

2. The Lord *restores* that which has been lost! (See Leviticus 25:25.)

3. The Lord *is* the Divine Protector! (See Numbers 35:19.)

4. The Lord *blesses* the family name! (See Deuteronomy 25:5-10.)

We discover that God is interested in persons, property, and posterity. It is time to wash yourself, anoint your head, and put on your best garments! Awakening and transforming revival demands renewed surrender and submission to the will of the Lord. He has not invited us to a weekend meeting. He is inviting us into the place of abiding, intimate fellowship with Him so he can deliver, restore, protect, and bless us.

In Jeremiah 32 the people repented before God, returned to Him with their whole hearts, and He returned to them in promise and power!

1. He gathered them and restored them (Jer. 32:36-37).

2. They received a new heart and mind to worship God (Jer. 32:38-39).

3. They were given an everlasting covenant (Jer. 32:40-42; 33:19-26).

4. They experienced great joy and exuberant singing (Jer. 33:10-11).

5. They enjoyed great prosperity (Jer. 32:43-44; 33:6-9, 12-14).

6. They would be ruled by the Messiah, the Son of David (Jer. 33:15-18).

The Fear of the Lord

How great the need to humble ourselves under the weightiness of His manifest glory and an understanding of His greatness and power! There are amazing attributes in the life of a believer who has revelation of the fear of the Lord. Those who fear the Lord:

- Afford pleasure to God (Ps. 147:11)
- Are pitied by God (Ps. 103:13)
- Are accepted by God (Acts 10:35)
- Receive mercy from God (Ps. 103:11,17; Luke 1:50)
- Are blessed (Ps. 112:1; 115:13)
- Confide in God (Ps. 115:11; Prov. 14:26)
- Depart from evil (Prov. 16:6)
- Converse together of holy things (Mal. 3:16)
- Should never fear man (Isa. 8:12-13; Matt. 10:28)
- Have their desires fulfilled by God (Ps. 145:19)
- Have their days prolonged (Prov. 10:27)

The fear of the Lord prepares the heart for a massive infilling of His mercy and power. The fear of the Lord shifts the atmosphere and shakes nations. The fear of the Lord renews intimate worship and reestablishes the throne of God in our midst. Watch the generations lie at the feet of Jesus in beautiful abandonment and the fear of the Lord lavishly baptize their hearts afresh in His sacred love. Let us rend our hearts like an old garment again before the Father. Let's believe Him for holy encounters, mighty dreams and visions, and a massive breakthrough in the Spirit that ushers in America's greatest awakening!

The Faith Renewed

We must govern the Kingdom of God into the earth by the Holy Spirit's intimate and authoritative worship. Our worship ushers in the dynamic revelation of heaven, but we must remember our worship is not just for intimacy but to receive revelation and release Kingdom authority upon the earth (see Matt. 6:9-13; 16:19; 18:18). We are seated with Christ in heavenly places and ruling on the earth from that realm (see Eph. 2:1-10).

The Lord is restoring the Church as His Ekklesia ,producing awakening and reformation. The awakening includes the arising of pioneers who will champion His cause in the earth, and the reformation includes the disciplines of Kingdom-minded strategists and missiologists. This restoration movement is not just for the reestablishing of intimate and authoritative worship, but restoration of biblical revelation to govern from the realm of heaven by the witness of the Holy Spirit.

The renewal of faith includes releasing the strategy of heaven. This strategy often cuts across the grain from the more readily accepted trends of modern culture and society. The truth is, prayer and fasting are a remarkable strategy of heaven that yields transformative fruit in this or any age. The strategy of heaven brings the Church to a place of rapid expansion and growth. Awakening brings expansion, not extinction.

The Strategy of Heaven: Ezra 1–5

Let's briefly consider some powerful truths from Ezra 1–5. These chapters describe four key events in the history of the remnant of Israel that had returned to their land.

Returning to the Land (Ezra 1–2)

No surprises here! It was nearly a millennium earlier when the exile and return were foretold when God entered into a covenant with Abraham (see Gen. 12:1-3). In fact, God had promised Abraham a land (Canaan), a seed (descendants as numerous as the stars in the heavens), and a blessing (blessing for Abraham and his descendants, and through his seed, blessing for all the families of the earth). We are living in the days of the covenant promise of God! His redemptive plan continues to unfold faithfully generation after generation.

We are stepping into the storyline of God's history and seeing His marvelous work in the hearts and lives of ordinary men and women. (See also Genesis 15:12-17; Isaiah 43:1-3,14-17; 44:27.)

Rebuilding the Temple (Ezra 3)

Ezra 3 is a powerful picture of a new beginning in God. However, not everyone was impressed. The "priests and Levites and heads of fathers' households, the old men who had seen the first temple, wept with a loud voice when the foundation of this house was laid before their eyes, while many shouted aloud for joy" (Ezra 3:12). The sound of joy and the sound of weeping were so voluminous that one could not be distinguished from another. When the sound of awakening is heard throughout the land there will be those filled with great joy, and others will be weeping over the days that used to be. We are coming into a brilliant and bold new beginning as the sound of awakening is released.

Resisting the Enemy (Ezra 4)

Ezra 4:1 reminds us that the enemies of Judah and Benjamin heard that the building of the temple had begun in Israel. The enemy always seeks to undermine and vigorously oppose the advance of the Kingdom of God in the nations. History marks the diverse attacks the enemy employs against the Church in times of awakening and revival. The enemy wants to silence the sound of the awakening, and he will employ distractions to try and discourage people and so they will settle back into their old life. The enemy will entice people to back down, to be afraid, and to blame leaders when they are afraid to lead. Resist the enemy by:

1. Living a lifestyle of forgiveness and faith (see Matt. 18). The Bible never called us to "forgive and forget," but to forgive is to release and move forward. Forgiveness resolves the conflict in you by the power of God's grace and mercy.

2. "Submit therefore to God. Resist the devil and he will flee from you" (James 4:7; see also Eph. 6:10-20). In addition, we are to draw near to Him continually (see 1 Pet. 5:7-11).

3. Persevere in the face of every obstacle and every opposition by maintaining your own personal growth through worship and thanksgiving and prayer. Most importantly, never relinquish the pursuit of His company.

Resuming the Work (Ezra 5)

"[They] began to rebuild the house of God which is in Jerusalem; and the prophets of God were with them supporting them" (Ezra 5:2). The sunrise of hope is before us and the clarion call for the sound of awakening has been heard in the land. The journey before us is a bold and brilliant work in the Spirit that is carved in a narrow path of pursuit, not of a gathering, but of His glory manifested in the fearless hearts of the ordinary ones.

When history loses its urgency, people have the greatest tendency to live at the expense of the future.

The sound of singing like muffled raindrops on a tin roof can be heard in the distance. The heralds have their songs muted by the utterly chaotic noise of a confused generation, but make no mistake, they are singing still. They bear on the wings of their song the blessing of God's timing and His hand of providence working in the lives of ordinary men and women. The Lord Himself is coming with an unfurled banner in one hand and a flaming torch in the other, lighting the way for all who will soon be awakened in the morning of His greatest harvest. What a harvest it is sure to be! There is a revelation that leads to demonstration.

Let the wonder of His revelation grip our hearts so every barrier seeking to divide us will be consumed upon the altar of intercession. There is a generation emerging who is no longer willing to tolerate the indifference of the past and is crying out for America's awakening and transforming revival. Oh, how our hearts cry out for the power of God to fall upon His people, transforming hearts and lives once again!

Charles Finney, at a schoolhouse near Antwerp, New York, describes the conviction of God falling upon a people when He steps into the room: "An awful solemnity seemed to settle down upon [the people]; the congregation began to fall from their seats in every direction, and cried for mercy. If I had had a sword in each hand, I could not have cut them off their seats as fast as they fell. ...I was obliged to stop preaching."[5]

The Hebrides Revival of 1949–1952 is an amazing story of the heart of the Father being revealed. The stories of the Hebrides Revival have impacted the world and once again remind us that God uses ordinary men and women in amazing and miraculous ways. Some might rightly say that it began in the two elderly sisters Peggy and Christine. The sisters were 84 and 82 years old respectively with one being blind and the other terribly arthritic. Were these the likely candidates for God to use in a revival that would touch the world? In this Awakening Mosaic, we would give a resounding "*Yes!*" However, we also find others in the storyline of the Hebrides Revival as well—John, the local blacksmith who would retreat to his barn for prayer and would be the one praying when the house shook. Literally shook. Then there was the girl from Stornoway who had visions and dreams. It is recorded that every vision she had came to pass.

Finally, there is a firsthand account of the remarkable night the spirit of prayer and intercession came upon a young deacon in the church. One night there was a group of people kneeling in John's barn praying and pleading this promise, "I will pour water on him that is thirsty, floods upon the dry ground" when one of the young men sprang to his feet and read Psalm 24:

Who shall ascend the hill of the Lord? And who shall stand in his holy place? He who has clean hands and a pure heart, who does not lift up his soul to what is false and does not swear deceitfully. He will receive blessing from the Lord (Psalm 24:3-5 ESV).

The young man quietly closed his Bible and, looking down at the minister and the other office bearers, said, "It seems to be so much humbug to be praying as we are praying, to be waiting as we are waiting, if we ourselves are not rightly related to God." The young man, lifting both hands, prayed, "God, are my hands clean? Is my heart pure?" History records the young man got no further in his prayer as he fell abruptly to his knees and went into a trance on the floor. Now, the moment he fell to the floor the minister and all who had gathered in the barn that evening were gripped by conviction that a God-sent revival must be related to His holiness.

Are my hands clean? Is my heart pure? You can never accurately predict upon whom the Spirit of God might come, but you can be sure He will fall upon the hungry, the broken, and the contrite before Him in the place of prayer.

I trust the point is well received—when the manifest glory of His Spirit comes, you can never predict whom God might use for His amazing purposes. The wonder of His revelation is available to all who will receive it and respond to Him out of hunger and expectation. The Lord is coming as a Father to reveal the fierceness of His love and the fire of His holiness. Our Father, the King of Glory, is coming and He will reign forever and forever.

When we allow the Holy Spirit to bring definition to our dreams and utterance to our prayers, He will release the potential within us—the potential to be used mightily in the next great move of God. There is a remnant Church arising and ablaze with the fire of His holiness and the unfurled banner of the harvest in their eyes.

Oh Lord, revive us again!

Are you ready to take your place in the magnificent storyline of God's history?

Notes

1. Jayson Casper, "Forgiveness: Muslims Moved as Coptic Christians Do the Unimaginable," Christianity Today, April 20, 2017, https://www.christianitytoday.com/news/2017/april/

forgiveness-muslims-moved-coptic-christians
-egypt-isis.html.

2. Philip Jenkins, *The Lost History of Christianity* (New York, NY: HarperCollins, 2009), 228.

3. Ibid.

4. Ibid.

5. Arthur Wallis, *In the Day of Thy Power* (Fort Washington, PA: CLC Publications, 2010), 76.

About Rick Curry

Rick Curry and his wife Jennifer have served in ministry for nearly 40 years pastoring thriving churches and traveling full time in evangelism ministries including international ministry and church planting. Rick has seen his dream of "An Appeal to Heaven" be heralded around the world and is very confident that America's greatest awakening lies ahead of her and not behind her. Rick and Jennifer are currently traveling full time and ministering the fire of awakening wherever they minister.